RECIPES
Unplugged

NO mixers! NO food processors! NO gadgets needed!

RIVKY MANIES

judaica PRESS

Recipes Unplugged
© 2017 The Judaica Press, Inc.

ISBN: 978-1-60763-240-5

Editor: Nechama Leshinsky
Proofreader: Hadassa Goldsmith
Designer: Justine Elliott
Photos on pp. 56, 58, 68, 72, 123, 125, 131,
196, 215, 224, 256, 258, 261, 262, 266 by:
    Jerry Deutsch
    jerry@photography-by-jerry.com
    photography-by-jerry.com
    Food styling by: Michael Giletto

Distributed by:
THE JUDAICA PRESS, INC.
123 Ditmas Avenue / Brooklyn, NY 11218
718-972-6200 / 800-972-6201
info@judaicapress.com
www.judaicapress.com

Manufactured in China

Contents

Since Yom Tov is one of those situations this cookbook is ideally suited for,
we include below some helpful halachic guidelines for Yom Tov cooking:

CONCISE LAWS OF COOKING ON FESTIVALS

(REPRINTED WITH PERMISSION FROM RABBI EHUD ROSENBERG, EXCERPTED FROM HIS BOOK, *LAWS OF COOKING ON THE SABBATH AND FESTIVALS*)

1. a. One may cook and bake on a festival as long as one intends to eat some of the food on the same day.

    b. It is, on the other hand, forbidden to cook and bake on a festival for the next day, whether that day be
       1) an ordinary weekday, or
       2) the second day of the festival.

2. a. Food whose taste will not deteriorate if it is cooked on the day before the festival (for example, fruit soup) should be prepared before the festival.

    b. If, however, through forgetfulness or lack of time, this was not done, one may prepare it on the festival, provided one introduces some variation into the normal method employed.

    c. No such variation is necessary if the food could not have been prepared before the festival, either
       1) due to there having been no physical possibility of doing so, or
       2) due to its being required on the festival for unexpected guests.

3. a. It is permissible to cook a pot full of meat on a festival, even though one needs only one piece, since the taste of the gravy is improved by the addition of more meat.

    b. This is so even if the additional meat not required for the festival is put into the pot when it is already standing on the fire, as long as one does not actually say that the additional meat is being cooked for after the festival.

4. Water may be heated, provided that the entire amount of water is put into the vessel at one time before it is put on the fire.

5. a. One should not, on a festival,
       1) bake or cook food for a non-Jew to eat,
       2) add food for a non-Jew to what one is baking or cooking for oneself, even in the same pot, nor
       3) invite a non-Jew to a meal (even if everything is ready), lest one come to cook additional food for him.

However, if this should lead to animosity or financial loss, it is permitted to give cooked food to the non-Jew provided that the food is not specially cooked for him but is cooked for one's consumption as well.

    b. On the Sabbath, on the other hand, it is permitted to invite a non-Jew to a meal.

    c. One is allowed, on a festival, to send food to a non-Jew that one has prepared for oneself on the festival or that was prepared before the festival, but only if

        1) the food is delivered by a non-Jew, or

        2) the existence of an *eruv* makes it permissible for the food to be delivered by a Jew.

    d. An exception is made in the case of a non-Jewish domestic (home-help) or servant, for whom one may add food to what one is cooking for oneself, but only

        1) in the same pot,

        2) before the pot is placed on the fire, and

        3) if one's relationship with the non-Jew is not such that one might come to cook for him or her separately.

6. It is permitted to use all types of installations for heating water, including those that have a thermostat, provided that one does not directly switch on the heating element. However, water heaters using gas, which are automatically switched on and off when the water tap (faucet) is opened or closed, may not be used, since extinguishing a flame on a festival is forbidden. (Such installations have a small "pilot" flame that burns continuously. Lighting the flame by opening the tap would be acceptable but closing the tap is not.)

7. It is permitted to use an electric stove that has been switched on before the festival, or even if it has been switched on automatically by a time switch during the festival. However, it is not permitted to switch the stove on or off manually or to change the heating level, since these actions usually involve connecting and disconnecting internal electrical heating elements.

PREPARING FOOD ON A FESTIVAL FOR THE SABBATH

1. It is not permitted to bake, cook, or prepare food on a festival for the next day, even if that next day is the Sabbath.

2. If the festival occurs on a Friday and one wishes to prepare food for the Sabbath on the festival, an *eruv tavshilin* should be performed before the commencement of the festival.

3. The *eruv* consists of setting aside a dish of cooked food and a piece of bread or matza. This is regarded as being the start of the preparation of the food for the Sabbath before the festival. Any further food preparation during the festival for the Sabbath is regarded as a continuation of the initial preparation that took place before the festival with the preparation of the *eruv*.

4. When preparing the *eruv*, the appropriate blessing should be recited.

5. If the head of the family prepares the *eruv*, members of the family are released from the obligation of individually preparing it. The same applies when two families eat at the same table, as long as each family does not eat its own food.

6. The dish of cooked food and the bread must be kept until the completion of cooking, baking, lighting, and other preparations one is making on the Friday before the Sabbath.

7. The preparation of the food on the festival should not be done late in the day, but well before the Sabbath commences. However, if a delay has taken place and hardship would otherwise be caused, one may cook and prepare food until shortly before the start of the Sabbath, all the more so on the second day of the festival.

8. When a festival of two days' duration occurs immediately prior to the Sabbath, the *eruv* is prepared earlier (immediately prior to the first day of the festival), but the actual cooking is done only on the second day.

Note

Since the issue of whether you need to check various types of fruits and vegetables for insects and precisely how to do so is somewhat complex, please consult your Rabbi.

Soups,
Salads,
and
Starters

Egg Drop Soup

SERVES 4

MEAT

YOU WILL NEED

2 qt. chicken soup (homemade or chicken broth)

2 T. soy sauce

4 eggs, beaten

4 scallions, chopped, to garnish

START COOKING

In a 6-quart pot, combine chicken soup and soy sauce and bring to a boil.
Remove from heat. Immediately stir in beaten eggs, whisking rapidly with
a fork to distribute eggs evenly, for about 30 seconds. Serve in bowls with
chopped scallions sprinkled on top.

*Swift and easy to prepare,
especially if using the extra
container of chicken soup you
have in the freezer!*

The Ultimate Chunky Vegetable Soup

YOU WILL NEED

Oil, for sautéing

2 onions, diced

4 carrots, diced

2 sweet potatoes, diced

4 celery stalks, diced

4 potatoes, diced

2 zucchini, diced

2 parsnips, diced

Water to cover vegetables, plus 5 cups

Salt, pepper, onion powder, and garlic powder, to taste

START COOKING

In a large pot, sauté onions until translucent, approximately 5 minutes. Add carrots, sweet potatoes, celery, potatoes, zucchini, and parsnips. Sauté all the vegetables for approximately 10 minutes. Add enough water to fully cover vegetables. Bring soup to a boil, lower the flame, and simmer for 1 to 2 hours covered. Add seasonings and at least 5 more cups water. Bring to a boil and then simmer for 10 minutes covered.

Chinese Chicken Corn Soup

YOU WILL NEED

4 c. chicken soup (homemade or chicken broth)

2 (14-oz.) cans cream-style corn

2 T. cornstarch

2 T. cold water

1–2 T. soy sauce

2 egg whites, lightly beaten

1 tsp. toasted sesame oil

Salt and pepper, to taste

4 scallions, chopped, to garnish

Tastes as good as the one you would order in a Chinese restaurant!

START COOKING

In a large saucepan, bring chicken soup and cream-style corn to a boil. Dissolve cornstarch in cold water and stir briskly into the boiling soup. Add soy sauce and simmer uncovered for 5 minutes or until thickened, stirring occasionally. Add beaten egg whites, slowly stirring all the while to evenly distribute the eggs in the soup. Stir in sesame oil and seasonings. Serve with chopped scallions as a garnish.

Easy to make, as you use shredded cabbage! Tastes super!

Cabbage Tomato Soup

YOU WILL NEED

1 (16-oz.) can tomato sauce

1 (15-oz.) pkg. shredded cabbage

2 T. lemon juice

2 T. sugar

2 tsp. salt

1 tsp. onion powder

¼ tsp. black pepper

1 lb. flanken (opt.)

Water, enough to cover

START COOKING

In a 6-quart pot combine all ingredients and bring to a boil. Turn down heat and simmer, covered, for 2 hours.

Creamy Pumpkin Soup

SERVES 8

PAREVE

YOU WILL NEED

2 (15-oz.) cans pumpkin

4 c. water

1 c. coffee creamer

1 garlic clove, minced

¼ c. maple syrup

2 T. margarine

Salt and pepper, to taste

Simple, original, and delicious!

START COOKING

In a 6-quart pot, bring first 4 ingredients to a boil. Lower heat and allow to simmer for 30 minutes, whisking often with a fork. Whisk in maple syrup and margarine and continue to simmer, covered, for 20 minutes. Add seasonings.

SERVES 10–12

PAREVE

Classic and wonderful!

Split Pea Soup

YOU WILL NEED

2 T. oil

1 lg. onion

2 garlic cloves, minced

2 celery stalks, diced

1 potato, diced

1 c. yellow and green peas, mixed

Water, to fill ⅔ of pot

2 tsp. salt

½ tsp. pepper

3 zucchini, peeled and diced

4 carrots, diced

1 sweet potato, diced

START COOKING

In an 8-quart pot, sauté onion, garlic, celery, and potato in oil for 20 minutes. Add peas and enough water to fill ⅔ of the pot. Bring to a boil, lower heat, and simmer for 2 hours, covered. Add remaining ingredients and cook for 1 hour, covered, on a low flame.

SERVES 8

PAREVE

A delicious, wholesome soup perfect for the winter!

Wholesome Potato Soup

YOU WILL NEED

1 T. margarine

1 lg. onion, diced

2 qt. water

⅓ c. split peas

3 potatoes, diced

2 carrots, sliced

2 celery stalks, diced

2½ tsp. salt

1 c. extra-fine egg noodles

START COOKING

In a 6-quart pot, melt margarine over medium/high heat. Add onion and sauté until translucent, approximately 5 minutes. Add all remaining ingredients except the noodles, and simmer for 2 hours, covered. During the last 30 minutes, add noodles.

Hearty Broccoli Soup

YOU WILL NEED

9 c. water

1 c. split peas

¼ c. barley

4 marrow bones

1 potato, diced

2 carrots, diced

1 onion, diced

4 T. onion soup mix

½ (24-oz.) bag frozen broccoli cuts

START COOKING

In an 8-quart pot, combine all ingredients except for the broccoli and simmer for 2½ hours. Add broccoli during the last 30 minutes.

The Best Caesar Salad

APPROX 10 SERVES

PAREVE

YOU WILL NEED

2 (8-oz.) bags Romaine lettuce
1 box cherry tomatoes, halved
1 c. large salad croutons

Dressing:

3 garlic cloves, minced
1 c. mayonnaise (you can use low-fat)
¼ c. sugar
¼ c. vinegar
¼ c. water
1 tsp. salt
⅛ tsp. pepper

Nothing beats a fresh, crisp Caesar salad, and there is no better recipe than this! An incredible dressing — double it; it keeps in the refrigerator for weeks!

LET'S GET STARTED

In a small bowl, whisk all dressing ingredients together with a fork. In a large bowl, toss together all salad ingredients and dressing (you do not need to use all of it!). Add croutons just before serving.

Cranberry Lettuce Salad

YOU WILL NEED

1 bag lettuce

1 c. dried cranberries

½ c. caramelized pecans

1 red onion, thinly sliced

Dressing:

5 T. mayonnaise

2 T. vinegar

1 T. sugar

½ tsp. garlic salt

LET'S GET STARTED

In a small bowl or cruet jar, mix all dressing ingredients until thoroughly combined. Place salad into a large bowl and toss together with dressing.

Edamame Couscous Salad

YOU WILL NEED

1 c. couscous (tiny grains), cooked according to pkg. directions

1 pkg. frozen shelled edamame, defrosted

1 red pepper, diced

1 yellow pepper, diced

1 red onion, diced

Dressing:

½ c. olive oil

¼ c. vinegar

1 T. Dijon mustard

2–3 T. of sugar

1 tsp. salt

Pepper, to taste

LET'S GET STARTED

In a large bowl, combine couscous, edamame, red pepper, yellow pepper, and red onion. Combine all dressing ingredients and add to bowl, tossing to combine. Serve at room temperature. Keeps well in the refrigerator for 2 to 3 days.

Quinoa is an excellent substitute!

Double Mushroom Sushi Salad

YOU WILL NEED

1 T. olive oil

4 Portobello mushrooms, washed
  and sliced into strips

1 garlic clove, minced

Salt and pepper, to taste

2 bags Romaine lettuce

1 red onion, sliced

1 (10-ox.) box white mushrooms,
  washed and sliced

1 English cucumber, sliced

2 avocados, diced

3 c. cooked sushi rice

Sesame seeds, for garnish

Dressing:

1 c. mayonnaise

¼ c. soy sauce

½ c. teriyaki sauce

¼ tsp. garlic powder

¼ tsp. onion powder

¼ tsp. paprika

*This salad is particularly
handy for when one has to
prepare an hors d'oeuvre in
advance. Everything can be
plated beforehand, and the
dressing and garnish can
be drizzled on whenever you
are ready to begin!*

LET'S GET STARTED

In a 9x13-inch pan, combine olive oil, Portobello mushrooms, garlic, salt, and
pepper. Bake uncovered at 350° for 30 minutes or until mushrooms begin
to shrink and become soft. Remove from oven and allow to cool to room
temperature.

In a large bowl, combine lettuce, red onion, white mushrooms, cucumber,
avocado and cooked Portobello mushrooms. Place a portion of salad on each
serving dish. Combine dressing ingredients. Add approximately ½ c. sushi rice
on top of the salad and drizzle dressing generously across the plate. Sprinkle
sesame seeds to garnish.

Meat and Angel Hair Salad

So delicious and kid-friendly, you won't have a morsel left!

YOU WILL NEED

1 c. mayonnaise

½ c. sugar

¼ c. vinegar

¼ c. water

1 tsp. salt

¼ tsp. pepper

1 tsp. yellow mustard

2 (8-oz.) salad bags (Euro or Romaine)

1 pkg. angel hair pasta, cooked according to pkg. directions

½ lb. corned beef, cut into short thin strips

½ c. yellow mini croutons

LET'S GET STARTED

In a medium-size bowl, using a metal fork, whisk together mayonnaise and sugar until smooth. Add vinegar, water, salt, pepper, and mustard, whisking vigorously after each addition. Divide lettuce among the salad plates. Place approximately 1 c. angel hair pasta on top and add meat strips on top of pasta. Drizzle dressing across the salad and top with croutons immediately before serving.

PAREVE

Delicious — no other way to describe it!

Toasted Sesame Mushroom and Lettuce Salad

YOU WILL NEED

1 (8-oz.) bag Romaine lettuce

2 red peppers, sliced into thin strips

1 (10-oz.) box mushrooms, washed and sliced into thin strips

½ c. sesame seeds

Dressing:

⅓ c. lemon juice

⅓ c. oil

¼ c. brown sugar

2 T. soy sauce

¼ red onion, diced

LET'S GET STARTED

Combine all salad ingredients in a large bowl. Place all dressing ingredients in a cruet jar or a small bowl and mix until thoroughly combined. Pour dressing over salad just before serving and toss until fully coated.

Nish Nosh Salad

YOU WILL NEED

1 pkg. B & B sour cream and onion
   crackers
1 (8-oz.) bag Romaine lettuce
1 red onion, sliced into rounds
1 box grape tomatoes
½ bag shredded white cabbage

Dressing:
½ c. water
½ c. oil
3 T. mayonnaise
4 T. sugar
1 tsp. salt
1 tsp. soy sauce
1 tsp. mustard
⅛ tsp. black pepper

LET'S GET STARTED

Place salad ingredients in a large bowl; toss to combine. Put all dressing ingredients in a cruet jar and shake vigorously until combined, or whisk together with a fork in a small bowl. Just before serving, combine dressing with salad.

APPROX 8 SERVES

PAREVE

Crunchy and yummy!

Tomato Salad

YOU WILL NEED

4 plum tomatoes, sliced
1 sm. onion, thinly sliced
2 T. olive oil
1 tsp. salt
⅛ tsp. pepper
1 tsp. garlic powder

LET'S GET STARTED

In a large bowl, combine all salad ingredients. Keep refrigerated.

APPROX 4 SERVES

PAREVE

APPROX 8 SERVES

MEAT

Elegant and mouthwatering!

Mushroom Pastrami Salad

YOU WILL NEED

1 (10-oz.) box mushrooms, washed and sliced

1 tsp. salt

⅛ tsp. pepper

1–2 T. olive oil

1 (8-oz.) bag Euro or Romaine lettuce

1 box grape tomatoes, halved

1 sm. red onion, thinly sliced

½ lb. pastrami, cut into long strips

Dressing:

1 garlic clove, minced

1 tsp. garlic powder

4 T. sugar

⅓ c. vinegar

¼ tsp. black pepper

⅓ c. olive oil

¼ tsp. salt

LET'S GET STARTED

Place mushrooms in a 9x13-inch pan. Season with salt and pepper and drizzle with olive oil. Place in oven and cook for 20–25 minutes at 350°. In a small bowl or cruet jar, combine all dressing ingredients. In a large bowl, place lettuce, tomatoes, cooked mushrooms, and onion, and toss to combine.

To serve: Divide the salad among the salad plates and place pastrami strips across the top. Drizzle dressing over salad.

The Winning Coleslaw

YOU WILL NEED

4 heaping T. mayonnaise

¼ c. vinegar

½ c. sugar

1 (14-oz.) bag coleslaw mix

LET'S GET STARTED

In a large bowl, whisk together mayonnaise, vinegar, and sugar with a fork (does not have to be perfectly blended). Add coleslaw and mix well until thoroughly combined. Allow to sit for 30 minutes. Keeps well in the refrigerator for at least a week.

After trying sooo many different versions of coleslaw, this one got the medal! The vinegar keeps this fresh for extra long!

Pretty Rotini Pasta Salad

AT LEAST 10-12 SERVES

PAREVE

A tasty and beautiful salad!

YOU WILL NEED

Dressing:
1 c. vinegar
½ c. oil
1 c. sugar
½ tsp. salt
½ tsp. pepper

1 lb. tri-color rotini pasta, cooked
 according to pkg. directions
1 red onion, diced
1 red pepper, diced
1 green pepper, diced
Fresh baby spinach leaf, for garnish

LET'S GET STARTED

In a medium pot over medium/high heat, boil all dressing ingredients. Lower heat and simmer for 5 minutes. Allow to cool. Combine pasta, onion, and peppers in a large bowl. Add dressing and mix well. Keeps in the refrigerator for at least a week. Add fresh baby spinach leaf to garnish.

APPROX
6–8
SERVES

PAREVE

Looks so pretty and pink!

Hearts of Palm and Beets Salad

YOU WILL NEED

1 can whole hearts of palm

1 can whole beets

1 tsp. garlic powder

2 tsp. olive oil

LET'S GET STARTED

Remove vegetables from cans and cut into small chunks. In a medium-size bowl combine hearts of palm, beets, garlic, and olive oil.

AT LEAST
12
SERVES

PAREVE

A magnificent salad that can be used as a centerpiece.

Stunning Vegetable Trifle Salad

YOU WILL NEED

1–2 (15-oz.) cans corn niblets
   (depending on size of trifle bowl)

1 (8-oz.) bag lettuce

1 red pepper, cut into strips

1 green pepper, cut into strips

1 (8-oz.) bag purple cabbage

1 orange pepper, cut into strips

1 box grape tomatoes, halved

1 c. pine nuts

Dressing:

4 T. mayonnaise

⅔ c. red wine vinegar

2 pkgs. dried Italian dressing

LET'S GET STARTED

Whisk all dressing ingredients in a small bowl with a metal fork until thoroughly combined; place in refrigerator. Layer trifle in order of ingredients, omitting the pine nuts. Pour dressing over trifle (dressing will seep down through the layers). Top with a layer of pine nuts.

Crunchy Leek Salad

YOU WILL NEED

2–3 leeks, diced (white part only)

1 box grape tomatoes

1 lemon

3 T. mayonnaise

1 T. sugar

1 tsp. salt

⅛ tsp. pepper

1 c. salted cashew nuts

LET'S GET STARTED

In a large bowl, combine leeks and tomatoes. Squeeze lemon over leeks and tomatoes. In a small bowl, combine mayonnaise, sugar, salt, and pepper and mix well. Pour over leeks and tomatoes and toss to thoroughly combine. Add cashew nuts just before serving.

Leeks are part of the onion family but nowhere near as sharp tasting; this salad is bursting with flavor!

Crunchy Asian Style Coleslaw

YOU WILL NEED

1 bag coleslaw mix

4 celery stalks, sliced

2 scallions, chopped

½ red onion, diced

½ c. toasted slivered almonds

1 c. chow mein noodles

Dressing:

¼ c. white vinegar

¼ c. sugar

1 T. soy sauce

2 tsp. sesame oil

½ c. olive oil

LET'S GET STARTED

In a small pan over medium/high heat, combine all dressing ingredients. Simmer until sugar is fully dissolved. Set aside to cool. In a large bowl, toss together coleslaw, celery, scallions, onion, and almonds. Add dressing and mix well. Just before serving, add the chow mein noodles.

Tomato Basil Pasta Salad

Bursting with flavor, this pasta salad is fabulous! You must use both dry and fresh basil; do not substitute one for the other!

YOU WILL NEED

5 cubes basil, defrosted, or 10 basil leaves, chopped

2 tsp. balsamic vinegar

2 T. ketchup

7-oz. bottle Thousand Island dressing

2 cubes minced garlic, defrosted, or 2 garlic cloves, chopped

1 tsp. oil

1 tsp. salt

⅛ tsp. pepper

1–2 T. dried basil

1 lb. pasta (rotini, penne, or small shells work well), cooked according to pkg. directions

1 box cherry tomatoes, halved

LET'S GET STARTED

In a large bowl, whisk together all ingredients except pasta and tomatoes. Add pasta and tomatoes and mix until thoroughly combined.

Outrageous Arugula Asparagus Quinoa Salad

This salad is absolutely divine!

YOU WILL NEED

Olive oil, for sautéing

1 (10-oz.) box mushrooms, washed and cut into chunks

1 bunch asparagus, washed and checked, cut into chunks

2 c. quinoa, cooked according to pkg. directions

1 lg. or 2 sm. containers arugula

Seeds of 1 pomegranate

Dressing:

¼ c. red wine vinegar

2 T. balsamic vinegar

1 T. soy sauce

Salt and pepper, to taste

LET'S GET STARTED

In a large skillet, sauté mushrooms and asparagus over medium/high heat until tender. Whisk together dressing ingredients in a small bowl using a metal fork or shake in a container with a tight-fitting lid. Combine dressing and vegetables with quinoa and arugula and serve with pomegranate seeds sprinkled on top.

A bright, crunchy, delightful salad — beautiful to look at and delicious to eat!

Sugar Snap Pea and Mango Salad

YOU WILL NEED

1 lb. sugar snap peas

8 oz. dried mango

4 scallions, chopped

1 onion, sliced

1 c. toasted almonds (slivered, sliced, or chopped)

Dressing:

½ c. Italian dressing

2 T. honey

1 T. mustard

LET'S GET STARTED

Combine all dressing ingredients in a small bowl with a metal fork or shake in a jar with a tight-fitting lid. In a medium-size bowl, mix together sugar snap peas, mango, scallions, onion, and almonds. Pour dressing over salad and toss to combine.

This is a handy recipe that can be used in several dishes!

Easy Crepes

YOU WILL NEED

4 eggs

2½ c. flour

1 c. water or pareve milk

½ tsp. salt

4 T. oil

Cooking spray oil, for frying

LET'S GET STARTED

In a medium-size bowl, combine all crepe ingredients and whisk briskly with a metal fork until thoroughly combined and very few lumps remain. Refrigerate mixture for 1–2 hours. Coat an 8-inch skillet with cooking spray oil and heat until hot enough that you can't place your hand past 6 inches above pan. Pour in ¼ c. batter and swirl swiftly until a thin layer fully coats the bottom of the pan. Turn crepe over when top looks dry, around 1–2 minutes; fry an additional 1–2 minutes and set crepes aside.

Sweet Potato Malawach Roll-Ups with Orange-Honey Sauce

YOU WILL NEED

1 pkg. frozen malawach

Filling:

1 (28-oz.) can sweet potatoes, drained and mashed

1 med. onion, diced and fried

½ tsp. salt

Dash of pepper

2 eggs

1 T. flour

Sauce:

½ c. fresh orange juice

½ c. white sweet wine

2 T. honey

A magnificent gourmet starter!

Tip: If you do not have sweet white wine, use dry wine and add ½ c. sugar!

START COOKING

In a medium-size bowl, combine filling ingredients and mix well. Allow malawach to defrost slightly. Cut pieces into 8 triangles and spread filling on each triangle. Roll up jelly-roll style, starting from larger end. Place on a greased cookie sheet. Bake at 350° for 30–40 minutes or until lightly brown.

For sauce: In a small pan, combine all sauce ingredients and whisk together with a metal fork. Over medium/high heat, bring mixture to a boil. Reduce heat and simmer uncovered for approximately 30 minutes or until sauce is reduced to half. Cool to room temperature. Serve 2 pieces per plate, with a little sauce drizzled across the plate.

Sweet & Sour Chicken Crepes

YOU WILL NEED

Filling:

Oil, for sautéing

½ c. fried onions

½ (10-oz.) box mushrooms, washed and diced, or 1 (8-oz.) can

1 red pepper, diced

1 green pepper, diced

1 lb. chopped ground chicken

1 tsp. salt

1 tsp. vinegar

1 tsp. paprika

1 beaten egg, for glazing

Sesame seeds

Sauce:

¼ c. fried onions

1 c. ketchup

¾ c. water

2 T. oil

⅔ c. sugar

1 pkg. frozen crepes, warmed or 1 Easy Crepes recipe — see p. 39

START COOKING

To make filling: In a large skillet, heat oil over medium/high heat. Add fried onions, mushrooms and peppers and sauté for 5 minutes. Add chopped chicken and break up into tiny pieces using a fork. Add salt, vinegar, and paprika and allow to cook until chicken has turned white, about 20 minutes.

To make sauce: While chicken is cooking, in a small pan heat all sauce ingredients, stirring briskly. Remove from heat.

To assemble: Place 1–2 T. of filling in the middle of each crepe. Fold left and right sides in, and then top and bottom over. Place seam-side down in a greased 9x13-inch pan. Brush with egg and sprinkle with sesame seeds. Bake uncovered at 350° for 20 minutes. Serve on individual plates with sauce drizzled generously over crepe. Serve warm.

SERVES 8

MEAT

This will be a big hit! The chicken toasts are crunchy, tasty, and awesome alone or paired with a crisp salad! You can use a cookie cutter to experiment with different shapes!

Crispy Chicken Sesame Toasts

YOU WILL NEED

1 lb. chopped ground chicken

1 egg, beaten

2 garlic cloves, minced

1 tsp. salt

⅛ tsp. pepper

1 loaf white bread, crusts removed

1½ c. sesame seeds

Oil, for frying

START COOKING

In a medium-size bowl, combine chicken, egg, garlic, salt, and pepper and mix well. Spread mixture evenly over slices of bread, right to the edge. Place sesame seeds on a plate and press chicken top side of each slice into seeds to coat evenly. Using a sharp knife, cut into quarters. In a wide skillet, heat ½ inch of oil until very hot. Add bread squares, chicken side down, and fry 3 minutes until lightly browned. Turn over and fry for an additional 1–2 minutes. (Keep an eye on them, as they cook quickly.) Drain toasts on paper towels and serve on a lightly dressed lettuce salad.

This freezes very well! Just remove from freezer and place on a cookie sheet. Heat in oven at 350° for 10 minutes or until heated through.

Beef and Broccoli Teriyaki

YOU WILL NEED

Sesame oil, for frying

2 fresh garlic cloves, chopped

1 lb. pepper steak

1 pkg. frozen broccoli florets

¼ c. water

2 T. cornstarch

¼ c. teriyaki sauce

1 tsp. salt

2 T. sesame seeds

This is an absolutely great tasting dish!

START COOKING

In a large skillet, heat oil over medium/high heat and sauté garlic until fragrant. Add meat and fry for 10–15 minutes or until cooked through. Add broccoli and continue to cook until florets are tender. In a small bowl, combine water and cornstarch until smooth. Add teriyaki sauce and mix well. Add to skillet and mix well. Serve on individual plates over a bed of rice.

Potato Spinach Pinwheels

SERVES 8

PAREVE

These are pretty to look at but even better to eat!

YOU WILL NEED

2 c. mashed or instant potatoes

1 (16-oz.) pkg. frozen spinach, defrosted
    and excess liquid drained

6 T. margarine

2 lg. onions, diced

3 eggs

Salt and pepper, to taste

1 pkg. ready rolled puff pastry sheets
    (usually contains 2 sheets)

1 beaten egg, for glazing

Sesame seeds

START COOKING

In a large bowl, combine potatoes and spinach. Heat margarine in a skillet over medium/high heat. Add onions and fry until golden brown. Add to potatoes and spinach mixture and mix well. Add eggs, salt and pepper and mix until thoroughly combined. Unroll puff pastry and spread filling onto both sheets. Roll up jelly-roll style. Brush with beaten egg and sprinkle with sesame seeds. Cut logs into 1-inch pieces and place flat onto a greased baking sheet. Place in oven and bake at 350° for 30–40 minutes or until pastries are puffed and golden brown. (This tastes best when baked right before serving.)

Soups,
Salads,
and
Starters
⤫

Dairy

Cream of Broccoli Soup

APPROX **6-8** SERVES

DAIRY

YOU WILL NEED

1 onion, diced

½ stick butter

½ c. flour

½ tsp. salt

¼ tsp. pepper

1½ c. pareve chicken broth (or 3
tsp. pareve chicken soup mix
combined with 1½ c. boiling water)

1½ c. milk

1 c. broccoli florets, chopped
coarsely (if frozen, fully
defrost first)

1 c. shredded cheddar cheese

*If making this soup in
advance, add grated cheese
just before serving! Perfect
served with crusty bread or in
a bread bowl!*

START COOKING

In a large pot, sauté the onion in butter until translucent, approximately 5
minutes. Lower heat and stir in flour, salt, and pepper until smooth and bubbly.
Slowly pour in broth and milk, mixing vigorously as you do so. Continue to stir
as the mixture thickens. Add broccoli. Simmer, stirring constantly, until heated
through (add more milk if it is too thick). Remove from heat and stir in cheese
until it has fully melted.

APPROX 8-10 SERVES

DAIRY OR PAREVE

Minestrone Soup

YOU WILL NEED

6 garlic cloves, minced

¼ c. olive oil

2 lg. onions, diced

4 celery stalks, diced

4 carrots, diced

1 can kidney beans or beans of your choice

1 (14.5-oz.) can diced tomatoes

2 med. zucchini, diced

1 c. uncooked elbow macaroni
    or other small pasta

4 c. pareve chicken broth (or 4 tsp. pareve
    chicken soup mix combined with 4 c.
    boiling water)

Salt and pepper, to taste

½ c. grated Parmesan cheese (opt.)

START COOKING

In a large pot over medium/high heat, sauté the minced garlic in the oil until it begins to brown. Add onions, celery, and carrots and sauté 10–15 minutes, stirring continuously until vegetables are tender. Add beans, diced tomatoes, zucchini, uncooked pasta and chicken broth and heat until it reaches a boil. Reduce heat, and simmer covered for about 20–30 minutes or until pasta is tender. Season with salt and pepper. Sprinkle with Parmesan cheese (opt.) just before serving.

APPROX
6-8
SERVES

DAIRY

A filling, spectacular soup!

Creamy Corn, Potato, and Cheese Soup

YOU WILL NEED

4 T. butter

1 onion, finely chopped

2 potatoes, peeled and diced

8 T. all-purpose flour

1¼ c. milk

2 cans corn niblets, drained

1½ c. cheddar cheese

3 c. heavy cream

¼ tsp. garlic powder

¼ tsp. onion powder

¼ tsp. paprika

Salt and pepper, to taste

START COOKING

Melt the butter in a large pot. Add the onions and cook over low heat, stirring occasionally for 5 minutes or until softened. Add the potatoes and cook, stirring for 2–3 minutes. Sprinkle in the flour and cook, stirring for 1 minute. Remove the pan from the heat and gradually stir in the milk. Return the pan to the heat and bring to a boil, stirring constantly. Reduce the heat and let simmer for 5 minutes or until potatoes are tender. Add garlic powder, onion powder, paprika, salt, and pepper, and then stir in the corn, cheese, and heavy cream. Heat gently until the cheese has just melted.

Dairy Leek and Potato Soup

YOU WILL NEED

2 leeks, diced (white parts only)

3 T. butter

4 potatoes, peeled and diced

4 c. water

2 T. pareve chicken soup mix or 2 bouillon cubes

2 celery stalks, diced

Salt and pepper, to taste

½ c. milk

START COOKING

In a large pot, sauté leeks in butter for 10 minutes. Add potatoes, water, soup mix, celery, and seasonings and bring to a boil. Cover pot and simmer on a low flame for 30 minutes. Add milk. Simmer for 10 more minutes. Serve hot.

If you like a creamier texture, use a fork or potato masher to mash the vegetables slightly — not too much, though, as you still want the soup to be a little chunky.

DAIRY

If you like a creamier texture, use a fork or potato masher to mash the vegetables until the soup is thick and creamy.

Sweet Potato and Onion Soup

YOU WILL NEED

4 T. vegetable oil

4 med. sweet potatoes, peeled and diced

2 med. carrots, peeled and diced

2 lg. onions, diced

4 garlic cloves, crushed

5 c. vegetable stock

2½ c. unsweetened orange juice

2 c. low-fat plain yogurt

2 T. chopped fresh parsley (or 2 parsley cubes)

Salt and pepper, to taste

START COOKING

In a large pot over medium/high heat, heat the oil and sauté sweet potatoes, carrots, onions, and garlic for approximately 5 minutes or until softened. Add the vegetable stock and orange juice and bring to a boil. Reduce the heat, cover the soup and allow to simmer for 20–30 minutes or until sweet potatoes and carrots are tender. Season with salt and pepper. Stir in yogurt and parsley before serving. Serve warm.

Baked Potato Soup

YOU WILL NEED

⅔ c. butter or margarine

⅔ c. all-purpose flour

7 c. milk

4 lg. baking potatoes, baked or cooked, peeled and cubed

4 scallions, sliced

1¼ c. grated cheddar cheese

1 c. sour cream

¾ tsp. salt

½ tsp. pepper

A great recipe that is enjoyed by kids and adults alike!

START COOKING

In a large pot over medium/high heat, melt butter. Stir in flour and continue to mix until smooth. Gradually add milk, stirring continuously until thickened. Add potatoes and scallions. Bring to a boil, stirring continuously. Reduce heat and simmer for 10 minutes, covered. Add grated cheese, sour cream, salt, and pepper. Serve warm.

Tomato Ravioli Soup

This soup hits the spot — it's really a meal in one!

YOU WILL NEED

Oil, for sautéing

1 lg. onion, diced

1 can (48-oz.) tomato juice

2 c. water

½ c. sugar

1 tsp. salt

⅛ tsp. pepper

¼ c. grated Parmesan cheese

Ravioli:

1 pkg. frozen ravioli, cooked according to pkg. directions

START COOKING

In a pot over medium/high heat, sauté onion until translucent, approximately 5 minutes. Add tomato juice, water, sugar, salt, and pepper and bring to a boil. Reduce heat and simmer, covered, for 20–30 minutes. Stir in Parmesan cheese. Add cooked ravioli to soup and serve hot.

Dave's Individual Quinoa Salad

SERVES 4

DAIRY

YOU WILL NEED

1 c. quinoa, cooked according to
    pkg. directions

1 (8-oz.) bag Romaine lettuce

1 (5-oz.) box arugula

1 sweet potato, cooked, peeled,
    and diced

4 to 5 dried apricots, diced into
    small pieces

1–2 oz. feta cheese, crumbled

1–2 T. olive oil

LET'S GET STARTED

Arrange each plate with the salad green of your choice. Sprinkle quinoa over salad. Add sweet potato, dried apricots and feta cheese on top of the quinoa. Drizzle with olive oil.

The ingredients in this salad may sound like an odd combination, but each one truly complements the other and results in a fabulously sweet, salty, and crunchy salad! You can multiply this recipe for as many people as you like!

APPROX 8-10 SERVES

DAIRY

Fresh, crunchy, and wholesome!!!

Dairy Quinoa Salad

YOU WILL NEED

4 c. quinoa, cooked according to pkg. directions

4 plum tomatoes, diced

1 English cucumber, diced

½ c. grated Parmesan cheese

¼ c. olive oil

Salt and pepper, to taste

LET'S GET STARTED

In a large bowl, combine quinoa, tomatoes, cucumber, Parmesan cheese, and olive oil. Season with salt and pepper. Mix well.

Quick and Easy Greek Salad

YOU WILL NEED

1 (8-oz.) bag Romaine lettuce

4 Kirby cucumbers, peeled and diced

1 (19-oz.) can sliced black olives

1 sm. red onion, sliced

3 plum tomatoes, diced

2 oz. feta cheese, crumbled

2 T. oil

2 tsp. red wine vinegar

Salt and pepper, to taste

LET'S GET STARTED

In a large bowl, place lettuce, cucumbers, olives, red onion, tomatoes, feta cheese, oil, and red wine vinegar. Season with salt and pepper. Mix well to combine.

Dairy Cucumber Salad

YOU WILL NEED

2 med. cucumbers, peeled and thinly sliced

1 sm. red onion, thinly sliced

1 T. parsley

Dressing:

¼ c. sour cream

¼ tsp. mustard

2 T. fresh dill (or 4 frozen dill cubes, defrosted, or dry dill)

1 T. vinegar

1 T. sugar

1 T. milk

1 tsp. salt

⅛ tsp. pepper

A fantastic, refreshing, creamy cucumber salad!

LET'S GET STARTED

In a medium-size bowl, combine cucumbers, onion, and parsley. In a small bowl or cruet jar, mix together all dressing ingredients until thoroughly combined. Pour dressing over vegetables. Cover and chill for at least 1 hour in refrigerator before serving.

Mediterranean Quinoa Salad

YOU WILL NEED

3 c. quinoa, cooked according to pkg. directions

1 box cherry or grape tomatoes, halved

1 cucumber, peeled and diced

1 yellow pepper, diced

4 oz. feta cheese

Dressing:

⅔ c. rice vinegar

⅓ c. olive oil

Juice of ½ a lemon

1 T. dried dill

¼ c. minced basil

Salt and pepper, to taste

LET'S GET STARTED

In a small bowl or cruet jar, mix together all dressing ingredients. In a large bowl, combine quinoa, dressing, and vegetables and mix well. Crumble feta cheese on top. Serve at room temperature or straight from the refrigerator.

APPROX 8 SERVES

DAIRY

My Favorite Feta Cheese Salad

YOU WILL NEED

1 avocado, diced

2 (8-oz.) bags Romaine lettuce

2 tomatoes, diced

2 scallions, chopped

3 oz. feta cheese

Dressing:

1 garlic clove, minced

1 tsp. mustard

1 tsp. sugar

1 T. mayonnaise

2–3 T. red wine vinegar

¼ c. oil

LET'S GET STARTED

In a small bowl (or in a cruet jar or container with a tight-fitting lid), combine all dressing ingredients (you may still be left with tiny lumps from the mayonnaise). In a large bowl, mix avocado, lettuce, tomatoes, and scallions with the dressing. Place in a salad bowl and crumble feta cheese on top before serving.

SERVES 4

DAIRY

Quick and classy, this makes a perfect accompaniment to any dairy meal!

Caprese Salad

YOU WILL NEED

2 med. tomatoes

½ lb. fresh mozzarella cheese

1 tsp. salt

1 T. olive oil

5 fresh basil leaves

LET'S GET STARTED

Cut tomatoes into thick round slices, then slice mozzarella cheese into thick round slices. On a platter, alternate tomato and mozzarella slices. Sprinkle salt evenly over tomatoes and cheese and drizzle with olive oil. Scatter the basil leaves on top.

Variation: If you cannot find fresh basil, you can combine the olive oil with 4 frozen basil cubes (defrosted) and drizzle over the tomato and mozzarella slices.

This is a fantastic starter! It not only looks good but tastes out of this world!

Roasted Vegetable Wonton Cups

YOU WILL NEED

3 T. balsamic vinegar

2 tsp. olive oil

¼ c. minced fresh basil (or 8 cubes frozen basil, or 1 T. dried basil)

1 sm. eggplant, peeled and diced

1 med. red pepper, diced

1 sm. red onion, diced

1 sm. zucchini, diced

1 sm. yellow squash, diced

Cooking spray oil

24 mini wonton wraps, defrosted

Dressing:

¼ c. fat-free plain yogurt

2 T. low-fat mayonnaise

1 T. of minced fresh basil (or 3 cubes frozen basil, or 1 tsp. dried basil)

1 tsp. lemon juice (fresh is best)

START COOKING

In a large bowl, combine vinegar, oil, and basil. Add all vegetables and toss to coat. Place vegetables in a single layer on a greased cookie sheet. Bake uncovered at 350° for 40–50 minutes or until tender, stirring occasionally. Meanwhile, in a small bowl, combine all dressing ingredients. Press mini wonton wraps into greased mini muffin tins. Bake wonton wraps uncovered at 350° for 15–20 minutes or until golden brown. Serve wonton wraps, 2 to a plate, filled with the roasted vegetables and the dressing drizzled on top.

Fabulous Stuffed Mushrooms

These are ABSOLUTELY delicious!

YOU WILL NEED

1 lb. white mushrooms
2 T. minced onion
3 garlic cloves, minced
6 oz. butter
½ c. breadcrumbs
1 tsp. chopped parsley
1 T. grated Parmesan cheese
Fresh parsley, to garnish (opt.)

START COOKING

Remove stems from mushrooms and finely chop them. In a small bowl, combine mushroom stems, minced onion, and 2 of the minced garlic cloves. In a medium-size skillet, melt ½ the butter (3 oz.) over medium/high heat. Add mushroom stem mixture and sauté for 3–5 minutes or until softened. In a small bowl, combine breadcrumbs, parsley, and cheese. Stir into the mixture in the skillet. Place mushroom caps, top side down in a greased 9x13-inch pan. Place a small spoonful of the hot mixture into each mushroom cap. In a small pot over medium/high heat, melt the remaining butter and minced garlic clove together and sauté for 2 minutes. Pour over the stuffed mushrooms and bake uncovered for 20 minutes. Serve warm, garnished with the fresh parsley.

Deep-Fried Stuffed Shells

YOU WILL NEED

16 jumbo size pasta shells, cooked according to pkg. directions

2 eggs

1 (6.5 oz.) can tuna, drained and mashed

1 c. shredded cheddar cheese (opt.)

1 med. tomato, seeded and chopped

2 T. chopped scallions

½ tsp. dried basil

⅛ tsp. black pepper

1 T. water

1 c. breadcrumbs

Vegetable oil, for frying

To serve: Tartar sauce or sour cream

An excellent way to start a meal!

START COOKING

In a medium-size bowl, slightly beat 1 egg with a metal fork Add the tuna, cheese (opt.), tomato, scallions, basil, and pepper and mix well to combine. Stuff the cooked shells with the tuna mixture. In a small bowl, beat the remaining egg together with the water with a metal fork. Prepare the breadcrumbs on a flat plate. Dip each stuffed shell into the egg mixture and roll in the breadcrumbs. In a large skillet over medium/high heat, heat 2 inches of oil until hot but not smoking. Fry shells a few at a time in the hot oil for 1½–2 minutes or until golden brown. Drain on paper towels. Serve with tartar sauce or sour cream.

APPROX 10 SERVES

DAIRY

This is a fabulous hors d'oeuvre, guaranteed to please the most elegant palette and the most simple!

Ravioli in Cream Sauce

YOU WILL NEED

2 boxes of ravioli, cooked according to pkg. directions

3½ c. heavy cream

½ c. grated Parmesan cheese

2 T. flour

2 garlic cloves, minced

Salt and pepper, to taste

START COOKING

In a large pan over medium/high heat, bring 3 c. heavy cream to a boil. (Keep an eye on the pot as heavy cream tends to boil over!) Lower heat and add Parmesan cheese. Combine the remaining ½ c. heavy cream with the flour to make a thick paste. Add the paste to the pot and stir continuously to ensure no lumps are formed. Bring to a boil. Add garlic, salt, and pepper. Remove from heat. To serve, place 3 to 4 ravioli on each serving dish and generously cover with the cream sauce.

Breaded Mozzarella Sticks

SERVES 6

DAIRY

YOU WILL NEED

1 c. flour

2 c. breadcrumbs

4 eggs, lightly beaten

½ tsp. pepper

½ tsp. garlic powder

½ tsp. onion powder

½ tsp. salt

Oil, for frying

1 (12-ct.) pkg. string cheese

To serve: pizza sauce

START COOKING

In a medium-size bowl, combine flour, breadcrumbs, eggs, and spices and mix well to form a smooth mixture. In a large skillet over medium/high heat, heat the oil until hot but not smoking. Remove string cheese from plastic wrappers. Roll in batter until completely encased and immediately drop into the hot oil. Fry a few minutes on each side until golden and crispy. Carefully remove sticks with a slotted spoon and drain on paper towels. Serve with warm pizza sauce.

Sides

The Most Heavenly Noodle/ Broccoli Kugel

YOU WILL NEED

Noodle Mixture:

1 (16-oz.) pkg. med. egg noodles, cooked

1 c. fried onions

½ c. brown sugar

½ c. flour

1½ T. salt

½ tsp. pepper

½ c. oil

Broccoli Mixture:

2 (20-oz.) pkgs. frozen broccoli, defrosted

3 T. flour

3 T. margarine

1½ c. mayonnaise

1 c. water

2 T. chopped onion

6 eggs

Salt and pepper, to taste

START COOKING

Combine all noodle mixture ingredients and pour into four greased 8-inch round pans or two 9x13-inch pans. Combine broccoli mixture ingredients and pour on top of noodles. Bake uncovered for 1½ hours at 350°.

The title says it all — honestly!

Superb Lukshen Kugel

YOU WILL NEED

½ c. fried onions

12 oz. med. egg noodles, cooked

3 eggs

½ c. flour

1 T. salt

1 tsp. pepper

¼ c. oil

½ c. brown sugar

START COOKING

Mix all ingredients. Pour into greased 9-inch square pan. Bake uncovered at 350° for 40 minutes.

This kugel gets top reviews every time!

SERVES 8–10

PAREVE

So easy, so delicious!

Quick as a Wink Broccoli Kugel in a Pie Crust

YOU WILL NEED

1 (16-oz.) bag frozen broccoli, cooked and drained

2–3 eggs

2–3 T. mayonnaise

Salt and pepper, to taste

½ tsp. garlic powder

½ tsp. onion powder

1 pie crust, baked

¼ c. cornflake crumbs

START COOKING

Combine broccoli, eggs, mayonnaise, and seasonings and pour into pie crust. Sprinkle cornflake crumbs on top and bake uncovered at 350° for 45 minutes. This slices perfectly and freezes well, too! Just reheat in the oven for about 30 minutes before serving!

SERVES 8

PAREVE

For the health-conscious, this is quite low in fat and carbs!

Cauliflower Kugel

YOU WILL NEED

1 (16-oz.) bag frozen cauliflower, cooked and drained

4 eggs

1 onion, diced

2 tsp. salt

¼ tsp. pepper

3 T. oil

START COOKING

Mash cauliflower in a medium-size bowl and add remaining ingredients. Mix well. Pour into a well-greased 8-inch square pan and bake uncovered at 350° for 1 hour or until top is golden.

Oatmeal Berry Bake

APPROX
20
PCS.
SERVES
(ONE 9x13 PAN)

PAREVE

YOU WILL NEED

2 c. flour

2 c. oatmeal

1½ c. brown sugar

2 tsp. cinnamon

2 sticks margarine, melted

1 (16-oz.) can whole berry cranberry sauce

1 (20-oz.) can crushed pineapple, drained

START COOKING

In a large bowl, combine flour, oatmeal, brown sugar, and cinnamon. Add margarine and mix well. Pour half of oatmeal mixture into a lightly greased 9x13-inch pan. Combine cranberry sauce and pineapple and spoon over oatmeal mixture. Top with remaining oatmeal mixture. Bake uncovered for 45–55 minutes at 350°.

Tastes so much like the classic apple berry bake but a lot easier to prepare — no peeling or chopping involved! Looks pretty cut into squares and served in cupcake holders.

Sweet Potato Pie

8–10 SERVES

PAREVE

YOU WILL NEED

1 (28-oz) can sweet potatoes, drained and mashed

½ c. sugar

½ c. non-dairy creamer

¼ tsp. salt

1 tsp. vanilla extract

1 pie crust, baked

1 c. brown sugar

¾ c. flour

¼ c. margarine, melted

Variation: I bake mine in an oven-to-table pan and omit the pie crust.

START COOKING

Combine first five ingredients in a medium-size bowl and pour into pie crust.
Mix last three ingredients in a small bowl until crumbly. Sprinkle over pie. Bake
uncovered at 350° for 45 minutes.

Lokshen Kugel in a Flash

YOU WILL NEED

4½ c. water

1 stick margarine, melted

2 tsp. salt

1 tsp. pepper

1 c. sugar

1 (16-oz.) bag fine egg noodles, uncooked

3 T. brown sugar

3 T. oil

2 eggs, lightly beaten

START COOKING

Bring water, margarine, salt, pepper, and sugar to a boil and remove from heat. Add noodles, brown sugar, oil, and eggs and mix well. Pour into 2 greased 8-inch round pans or a greased 9x13-inch pan. Bake uncovered at 350° for 1 hour.

Any steps you can skip successfully when cooking are a bonus, so not having to drain the noodles is fantastic. So is the taste of this yummy kugel!

Pineapple Noodle Kugel

YOU WILL NEED

1 (16-oz.) bag fine egg noodles

2 sticks margarine, melted

1½ c. sugar

6 eggs

1 tsp. vanilla

1 (20-oz.) can crushed pineapple with juice

START COOKING

Cook egg noodles according to package directions. With a fork, whisk together remaining ingredients and mix with the noodles. Bake uncovered in a greased 9x13-inch pan at 350° for 1 hour or until golden.

A tantalizing noodle kugel that tastes almost dairy!

SERVES 10–12 SLICES

PAREVE

When sliced, it creates a pinwheel effect; the slices look and taste heavenly!

Onion Strudel

YOU WILL NEED

1 c. fried onions

1½ tsp. salt

⅛ tsp. pepper

1 egg

1 puff pastry sheet

1 egg yolk

START COOKING

In a small bowl, combine fried onions, salt, pepper, and egg and mix well. Unroll pastry sheet and spread onion mixture over dough. Roll up jelly-roll style and pinch edges closed; bring ends together to form a round circle and pinch closed. Place on well-greased cookie sheet or 9-inch round pan; brush with egg yolk. Cut small slits at 2-inch intervals along the circle. Bake uncovered at 350° for 1 hour or until golden brown.

Butternut Squash Pie

YOU WILL NEED

2 (12-oz.) boxes frozen winter squash, defrosted

7 egg whites

1 c. flour

1 c. sugar

¼ c. pareve milk

START COOKING

Mix all ingredients until thoroughly combined. Pour into greased 9x13-inch pan and bake uncovered at 350° for 1 hour.

You can also make these in muffin pans and pop them out to serve!

SERVES 8–10

PAREVE

*Super easy and freezes
excellently!*

Pumpkin Pie

YOU WILL NEED

¾ c. sugar

½ tsp. salt

1 tsp. ground cinnamon

2 lg. eggs

1 (15-oz.) can pumpkin

1 baked 9-inch deep-dish pie crust

START COOKING

Mix sugar, salt, and cinnamon in a small bowl. In a large bowl, beat eggs with a fork, and then add pumpkin and spice mixture. Mix vigorously until thoroughly combined. Pour into pie crust. Bake uncovered at 350° for 50 minutes.

Apple Kugel

YOU WILL NEED

10 apples, peeled and sliced
1 c. sugar
1 c. oil
6 eggs

2 c. flour
2 tsp. vanilla extract
½ tsp. baking powder
½ tsp. cinnamon

START COOKING

Put apples in a greased 9x13-inch pan. In a medium-size bowl, mix remaining ingredients until smooth. Pour over apples and bake at 350° for 1 hour or until top is golden .

You can serve this warm or at room temperature!

Broccoli Kugel

YOU WILL NEED

1 (16-oz.) bag frozen broccoli
    (not florets)
1½ T. flour
1½ T. margarine
3 eggs

½ c. mayonnaise
1 tsp. salt
¼ tsp. pepper
1½ c. cornflake crumbs

START COOKING

Cook broccoli according to package directions. If broccoli pieces are large, chop into smaller pieces. Combine all ingredients except cornflake crumbs in a medium-size bowl. Pour into 2 greased 8-inch round pans and sprinkle with cornflake crumbs . Bake uncovered at 350° for 1 hour or until top is golden.

Sweet Potato Kugel

YOU WILL NEED

3 med. sweet potatoes, peeled, cooked, and mashed

½ c. sugar

½ c. non-dairy creamer

¼ tsp. salt

1 tsp. vanilla extract

1 pie crust, baked

1 c. brown sugar

¾ c. flour

¼ c. margarine, melted

START COOKING

Combine first 5 ingredients in a medium-size bowl and pour into pie crust. Mix last 3 ingredients in a small bowl until crumbly. Sprinkle over sweet potatoes. Bake at 350° for 45 minutes.

Tzimmes

YOU WILL NEED

1 (24-oz.) bag sliced frozen carrots

1 sweet potato, diced

½ c. water (not more!)

½ c. honey

START COOKING

Combine all ingredients in a small pan. Simmer on a low flame for 2 hours.

10 SERVES

PAREVE

Once you try this method, you won't eat your green beans any other way!

Bright Green Crunchy Green Beans

YOU WILL NEED

2 lbs. fresh thin green beans

¼ c. olive oil

1½ tsp. salt

3 T. garlic powder

Olive oil cooking spray

START COOKING

Combine all ingredients in a large bowl. Spread green beans evenly onto a cookie sheet greased with cooking spray. Bake uncovered at 350° for no longer than 6 minutes. You can serve them at room temperature.

Zeli
(Sweet and Sour Purple Cabbage)

YOU WILL NEED

2 lg. onions, diced

Oil, for frying

1 head purple cabbage, shredded

1 T. paprika

2 tsp. salt

½ tsp. pepper

½ c. ketchup

¼ c. honey

This is an old recipe from pre-war Europe — still wholesome and enjoyed by all!

START COOKING

In a large pot, fry onions in oil until golden brown. Add shredded cabbage and sauté for 5 minutes. Add the rest of the ingredients and mix until thoroughly combined. Cook covered on low heat for 2 hours. Serve warm.

Green Beans in White Sauce

YOU WILL NEED

1 lb. green beans, fresh or frozen
6 c. water

Sauce:
4 T. flour
4 T. sugar
4 T. oil
4 T. vinegar
1 tsp. salt
1 c. reserved water

START COOKING

In a 6-quart pot, combine beans and water and bring to a boil. (For frozen, cook according to package directions.) Drain water, reserving 1 c. for sauce, and place beans in a 9x13-inch pan. Combine all sauce ingredients in small pot and mix vigorously over a low flame until smooth. Pour sauce over green beans; toss to coat evenly. Serve in a salad bowl or on a platter.

SERVES 8

PAREVE

A tasty way to dress your green beans!

Dressed Up Orzo

YOU WILL NEED

¾ c. orzo
⅓ c. chopped onion
1 T. oil
¼ c. craisins

¼ tsp. turmeric
1 tsp. salt
⅛ tsp. pepper

START COOKING

Cook orzo according to package directions; set aside in medium-size bowl. In a small frying pan, sauté onion in oil until translucent, approximately 5 minutes. Add craisins and sauté for another 5 minutes; add spices. Add to orzo and mix well. Serve warm.

SERVES 3-4

PAREVE

Turmeric adds a mysterious and dramatic yellow color to your foods; try this recipe — you will not be disappointed!

6–8 SERVES

PAREVE

Super easy to prepare!

Oriental Broccoli

YOU WILL NEED

1 (24-oz.) bag frozen broccoli florets

3 T. soy sauce

1 T. oil

3 tsp. sugar

Oil, for frying

6 garlic cloves, minced

START COOKING

Cook broccoli according to package directions. In a small bowl, combine rest of ingredients excluding the garlic. Heat oil in a medium-size frying pan. Add garlic and sauté for 30 seconds to 1 minute, stirring continuously. Add soy sauce mixture and broccoli to pan and continue to stir for another 2 minutes. Serve warm.

Marinated Roasted Vegetables

YOU WILL NEED

1 onion, cut into strips
1 (15-oz.) can baby corn
1 c. baby carrots, cut into strips
1 green squash, cut into strips
1 green pepper, cut into strips
1 yellow pepper, cut into strips
1 red pepper, cut into strips
3 c. snow peas

Dressing;

¼ c. brown sugar
¼ c. oil
⅓ c. soy sauce
2 T. vinegar
1½ tsp. garlic powder

Flavorful, crunchy, and tantalizing!

Tip: To prepare in advance, marinate vegetables in a Ziploc bag. Pour onto cookie sheet when ready to roast.

START COOKING

Mix vegetables and place on a greased baking sheet. Mix all dressing ingredients and pour over vegetables. Marinate for 30 minutes. Bake uncovered at 350° for 30 minutes.

Cauliflower Latkes

YOU WILL NEED

1 (24-oz.) bag frozen cauliflower
2 T. matzo meal
2 eggs

1 tsp. salt
⅛ tsp. pepper
Oil, for frying

START COOKING

Cook cauliflower according to package directions. Mash cauliflower and mix in remaining ingredients. Heat oil in a large frying pan. Drop spoonfuls of mixture into the hot oil and fry until golden on both sides. Serve warm.

These make a great alternative to traditional potato latkes but are no less scrumptious!

*The peppers add great color
to this dish!*

Potatoes and Peppers

YOU WILL NEED

1 lg. onion, sliced

1 red pepper, cut into chunks

1 green pepper, cut into chunks

1 yellow pepper, cut into chunks

8 red potatoes, scrubbed clean and
cut into small chunks

2 garlic cloves, minced

½ c. oil

1 tsp. salt

¼ tsp. pepper

START COOKING

In a large bowl, mix all ingredients together. Pour onto a greased cookie sheet, cover, and bake at 350° for 1½ hours; mix again and cook for another 30 minutes uncovered.

SERVES 8

PAREVE

Extremely tasty!

Roasted Mustard Potatoes

YOU WILL NEED

3 lbs. red potatoes, scrubbed clean
    and cut into quarters with skin on

3 T. olive oil

1½ tsp. salt

⅛ tsp. pepper

Sauce:

3 T. white wine vinegar

2 T. Dijon mustard

2 T. olive oil

Pinch of salt and pepper

START COOKING

In a large bowl, combine potatoes, olive oil, salt, and pepper. Pour onto a greased cookie sheet and bake uncovered at 350° for 2 hours. In a large bowl, whisk all sauce ingredients together with a fork. Add hot potatoes and toss to coat evenly. Serve warm or at room temperature.

Professional Caterer-Style Roasted Potatoes

YOU WILL NEED
5 cans whole potatoes, drained
½–¾ c. olive oil
Salt and paprika, to taste

START COOKING
Spread potatoes on a greased cookie sheet. Toss potatoes with oil, salt, and paprika and bake covered at 350° for 2 hours. Uncover and bake for another 2 hours, occasionally turning the potatoes .

The hardest part is opening the cans! These potatoes present beautifully and make it look like you are an executive chef!

Glazed Sweet Potatoes

YOU WILL NEED

6 med. sweet potatoes, peeled and cut into small chunks

1 stick margarine

1 c. brown sugar

½ c. orange juice

¼ c. oil

START COOKING

On a well-greased cookie sheet, place sweet potatoes in a single layer. Combine remaining ingredients in a small pot and bring to a boil. Pour over sweet potatoes and bake uncovered at 350° for 2½ hours, basting every 30 minutes.

No matter how big of a pan you make of these, there is never any left over. Hopefully you have enough to bring to the table!

Shake and Bake Potatoes

YOU WILL NEED

3 lbs. red potatoes, scrubbed clean and cut into small chunks

½ c. ketchup

¼ c. oil

1½ tsp. salt

1 tsp. garlic powder

1 tsp. paprika

START COOKING

In a large Ziploc bag, shake all ingredients until potatoes are evenly coated. Place potatoes onto a greased cookie sheet and bake uncovered at 350° for 2 hours.

These may disappear before the meal. (They also get eaten from the oven, so watch out!)

Roasted Red Potatoes and Sweet Potatoes

YOU WILL NEED

3 lbs. red potatoes, scrubbed clean and cut into chunks

4–6 sweet potatoes, peeled and cut into chunks

1 c. oil

1 T. salt

1 T. paprika

1 lg. onion, sliced

START COOKING

In a very large bowl, combine all ingredients. Pour onto a well-greased cookie sheet and bake uncovered at 350° for 2–2½ hours.

Cherry Squares

YOU WILL NEED

5 T. margarine, softened

1 c. flour

¼ c. sugar

1 tsp. baking powder

1 egg

½ (21-oz.) can cherry pie filling

START COOKING

Rub margarine into the flour. Add sugar and baking powder until it forms a crumbly mixture; reserve ½ c. of the crumbs. Add egg to mixture to form a soft dough and press dough into a well-greased 7-inch pan. Spread pie filling over dough. Sprinkle remainder of crumbs over filling and bake uncovered at 350° for 1 hour.

This can also be used as a dessert. If your family has a sweet tooth, serve as a side dish!

SERVES 8

PAREVE

Scalloped Potatoes

YOU WILL NEED

3 T. onion soup mix

6 potatoes, peeled and thinly sliced

½ stick margarine, melted

1 (16-oz.) container coffee creamer

START COOKING

In a medium-size bowl, combine all ingredients. Pour into a greased 8-inch square pan with the potato slices overlapping each other. Bake covered at 350° for 1 hour.

If not cooking on Yom Tov and you can adjust the oven setting, uncover and broil for 10 more minutes to make the top crispy.

Who knew that this could be made pareve? It tastes just like the dairy version and looks equally as good, too!

Spanish Rice

YOU WILL NEED

1 onion, thinly sliced

Oil, for sautéing

4 c. white rice, cooked

¼ c. craisins

¼ c. dry apricots, chopped

¼ c. roasted slivered almonds

Salt and pepper, to taste

START COOKING

Sauté onion in oil until translucent, approximately 5 minutes, and add to cooked rice. Combine with remaining ingredients. Serve warm.

This flavorsome rice dish is sweet and savory and perfect for a crowd!

Rice Pilaf

YOU WILL NEED

2 c. rice, uncooked

1 (4-oz.) can mushrooms (including the liquid)

¼ c. oil

3 T. soy sauce

3 T. onion soup mix

4 c. water

START COOKING

Combine all ingredients and pour into a greased 9x13-inch pan. Bake covered at 350° for 1 hour or until all water is absorbed.

No pot to wash out!

This not only looks good, it tastes great, too! Slices beautifully!

Layered Rice and Vegetables

YOU WILL NEED

2 c. rice, uncooked
1 onion, diced small
2 carrots, diced small
1 red pepper, diced small
1 (8-oz.) can mushrooms
½ c. oil
4 c. water
4 T. onion soup mix

START COOKING

Spread rice on bottom of a greased 9x13-inch pan. Layer vegetables as follows: onion, carrots, pepper and mushrooms. Boil oil, water, and onion soup mix in a small pan; pour over vegetables and rice. Bake at 350° for 1 hour covered and 15 minutes uncovered.

Great served with pepper steak or sweet and sour chicken.

Fried Rice

YOU WILL NEED

1 c. rice, uncooked
2 c. water
½ tsp. salt
2 T. soy sauce
2 scallions, sliced
Oil, for sautéing

START COOKING

Sauté rice in oil in a medium pot, stirring continuously. Add water, salt, soy sauce, and scallions and bring to a boil. Lower flame and simmer 20–30 minutes or until all water is absorbed.

This looks and tastes sensational!

Orzo Medley

YOU WILL NEED

1 onion, diced

Oil, for frying

1 (8-oz.) can mushrooms

1 can whole baby corn, sliced

1 red pepper, diced

2 c. sugar snap peas

1 (16-oz.) pkg. orzo, cooked

3 T. sesame oil

Salt and pepper, to taste

START COOKING

Sauté onion in oil until translucent, approximately 5 minutes. Add mushrooms, corn, pepper, and sugar snap peas and sauté until tender. Combine with orzo. Add sesame oil, salt, and pepper. Serve warm.

SERVES 8

PAREVE

An old-time favorite!

Kasha Varnishkes

YOU WILL NEED

1 egg

½ tsp. salt

⅛ tsp. pepper

1 c. kasha

3 c. boiling water or stock

1 lg. onion, diced and fried until golden

1 (16-oz.) box bowtie (farfalle) pasta, cooked according to pkg. directions

START COOKING

Beat egg with salt and pepper and stir into the kasha. Pour into a saucepan and stir over low heat to set the egg. Add boiling water or stock and cook until all the water has been absorbed and grains are tender. (You may need to add a little more water.) Combine kasha, noodles, and fried onions, adding more salt and pepper to taste. Serve warm.

No Cook Couscous Dish

SERVES 8–10

PAREVE

YOU WILL NEED

1⅓ c. couscous (tiny grains, uncooked)

4 tomatoes, chopped

1 green pepper, chopped

1 red onion, diced

½ cucumber, diced

1 garlic clove, minced

⅓ c. fresh parsley

¼ c. olive oil

1 tsp. salt

⅛ tsp. pepper

Juice of 1 lemon

START COOKING

In a large bowl, combine all ingredients except for the lemon juice. Pour lemon juice over salad and mix until thoroughly combined. Refrigerate for at least 2 hours. This will keep in refrigerator for at least 3–4 days.

What could be easier? Combine the raw couscous and you're done! I use tri-color couscous, but regular also looks pretty!

6–8
SERVES

PAREVE

Delicious served with rice!

Ratatouille

YOU WILL NEED

1 onion, diced

Oil, for frying

2 zucchini, diced

1 red pepper, diced

1 green pepper, diced

3 tomatoes, diced

1 sm. can tomato paste

START COOKING

Sauté onion in oil until translucent, approximately 5 minutes. Add remaining vegetables and sauté until tender. Add tomato paste and simmer on low heat for 1 hour.

Vegetable Lo Mein

YOU WILL NEED

2 onions, diced

6 garlic cloves, minced

Oil, for frying

1 red pepper, diced

1 (24-oz.) bag frozen broccoli

1 (24-oz.) bag frozen cauliflower

½ c. soy sauce

½ c. teriyaki sauce

1 (16-oz.) pkg. angel hair pasta, cooked

START COOKING

Sauté onions and garlic in a little oil for 5 minutes. Add remaining vegetables and stir fry 5–6 minutes; add soy sauce and teriyaki sauce. Continue cooking on low flame for 15 minutes. Combine angel hair pasta with vegetables. Serve warm.

A great recipe, using ingredients you have at home! It makes a lot, so it's perfect for a crowd!

12 SERVES

PAREVE

These are fabulous and freeze well!

Incredible Pumpkin Muffins

YOU WILL NEED

Muffins:

2 c. sugar

4 eggs

1 c. oil

1 tsp. vanilla extract

2 c. flour

2 tsp. baking powder

2 tsp. baking soda

1½ tsp. cinnamon

1 tsp. salt

1 (15-oz.) can of pumpkin

Topping:

1 c. Grape Nuts cereal

1 c. flour

¾ c. brown sugar

⅓ c. oil

START COOKING

In a large bowl, combine sugar, eggs, oil, and vanilla. Add flour, baking powder, baking soda, cinnamon, salt, and pumpkin and mix until smooth. Pour into greased muffin tins.

Topping: In a medium-size bowl, combine all topping ingredients and mix well. Sprinkle topping over each muffin. Bake at 350° for 30 minutes or until a toothpick comes out clean when inserted.

Cranberry Apple Kugel

SERVES 8

9X9 SQUARE

PAREVE

YOU WILL NEED

1 c. flour

1 c. oatmeal

1 c. brown sugar

¾ stick margarine

½ tsp. cinnamon

2 Macintosh apples, diced

1 can whole berry cranberry sauce

START COOKING

Mix flour, oatmeal, brown sugar, margarine, and cinnamon until it forms a crumbly mixture. Press ½ of crumbs into a greased 9x 9-inch square pan. Combine apples and cranberry sauce and spread on top of crumbs. Sprinkle with remaining crumbs. Bake uncovered at 350° for 1 hour.

You can serve this as a side dish or a dessert. Either way it is fabulous!

A scrumptious vegetable side dish made more substantial by the rice!

Vegetable Jumble

YOU WILL NEED

2 T. olive oil

2 garlic cloves, minced

1 red onion, sliced

1 eggplant, diced

1 green pepper, diced

1 (15-oz.) can baby corn, drained, cleaned, and sliced lengthwise

1 c. small broccoli florets

⅔ c. hot vegetable stock

1 (8-oz.) can chopped tomatoes

1 T. tomato paste

½ tsp. dried red pepper flakes (more if you like it spicy!)

Salt and pepper, to taste

½ c. rice, cooked

START COOKING

Heat oil in a large skillet over medium/high heat. Add garlic and onion and cook, stirring constantly for 2–3 minutes. Add eggplant, pepper, baby corn, and broccoli and cook for another 3–4 minutes, stirring occasionally. Stir in vegetable stock, tomatoes, tomato paste, red pepper flakes, salt, and pepper and cook over low heat for 15–20 minutes or until vegetables are tender. Add cooked rice to vegetables and heat, gently stirring for 3–4 minutes. Serve warm.

Garlic Spirals

YOU WILL NEED

1 pizza dough

½ c. olive oil

2 tsp. salt

3 frozen garlic cubes, defrosted

START COOKING

Divide pizza dough into 24 pieces. Roll each piece into a long rope. In a small bowl, combine olive oil, salt, and garlic and mix well. Using a pastry brush, brush garlic mixture evenly over each rope and roll into a spiral shape, tucking the end tightly underneath. Place spirals on greased cookie sheet and allow to rise for half an hour. Bake uncovered at 350° for 20 minutes or until golden brown.

A slightly more elegant presentation of the ever-popular garlic knot!

Onion Board

YOU WILL NEED

2 pizza doughs

4 T. olive oil

1 med. onion, diced very small

2 tsp. poppy seed (opt.)

START COOKING

Press pizza dough into 2 greased 9x13-inch pans. Brush dough with olive oil and evenly sprinkle onion on top. Let rise for 15 minutes. Place in oven and bake 25–35 minutes or until golden brown and puffed up. Cut into squares with a sharp knife or pizza cutter.

This is an invaluable recipe that is really worth doubling. It stores exceptionally well and is an ingredient that can be used in several dishes!

Homemade Pancake Mix

YOU WILL NEED

4 c. flour

3 T. baking powder

2½ tsp. salt

1 T. sugar

1 c. oil

START COOKING

Place all ingredients into a large bowl. Using your fingers, Combine the mixture together until it resembles fine breadcrumbs. Store in an airtight container or Ziploc bag. (The mixture will turn white and get hard if you freeze it; however if you allow it to defrost, it will return to its original state.)

Quick and Easy Good Hearty Bread

SERVES 6-8

PAREVE

YOU WILL NEED

3 c. flour
3 tsp. baking powder
1 tsp. salt

¼ c. sugar
¼ c. oil
1 (12-oz.) beer

START COOKING

In a medium-size bowl, mix together flour, baking powder, salt, and sugar. Add oil and beer and carefully mix to combine. Do not over mix! Place dough in loaf pan and bake uncovered at 350° for 1 hour. Remove from pan and cool for at least 20 minutes before slicing.

This bread is so delicious — crusty and golden on the outside and soft on the inside! A superb recipe with only a short preparation time!

Sides
&
Dairy

Asparagus Tartlets

YOU WILL NEED

Filling:

1 egg

1 egg yolk

⅔ c. milk

1 (16-oz.) bag frozen asparagus,
     cooked according to pkg. directions

½ tsp. salt

Pepper, to taste

½ c. grated Parmesan cheese

6 mini (3") tart shells, baked

A truly elegant side dish!

START COOKING

In a large bowl, use a metal fork to combine egg, egg yolk, and milk and mix until smooth. Add cooked asparagus, salt, pepper, and Parmesan cheese.

Fill each mini tart shell with asparagus filling. Bake 20 minutes uncovered until set and golden. Serve warm or at room temperature.

Overnight French Toast

DAIRY

YOU WILL NEED

¼ c. (half a stick) butter, room temperature

12 (¾-inch thick) French bread slices
    or leftover challah slices

6 eggs

1½ c. milk

¼ c. sugar

2 T. maple syrup

1 tsp. vanilla

½ tsp. salt

To serve: powdered sugar, maple syrup,
    cinnamon, sugar (opt.)

*A fantastic recipe that allows
you to have breakfast in the
morning without standing over
a hot frying pan!*

START COOKING

Spread butter evenly over a cookie sheet. Arrange bread or challah slices on top
of the butter. In a large bowl using a metal fork, beat eggs, milk, sugar, syrup,
vanilla, and salt. Pour mixture over bread. Turn bread slices over to coat. Cover
with plastic wrap and refrigerate overnight. Preheat oven to 350°. Bake uncovered
for 20 minutes. Turn bread over and continue baking until just golden, about 15–20
minutes more. Transfer French toast to serving plates and sprinkle with powdered
sugar and extra maple syrup, cinnamon, and sugar or topping of your choice!

Cheese Croquettes

YOU WILL NEED

1 c. fried onions

3 c. breadcrumbs

2 c. grated mozzarella cheese

5 eggs

1 tsp. garlic powder

⅛ tsp. salt

⅛ tsp. pepper

Cooking spray oil

To serve: marinara sauce, sour cream

START COOKING

In a large bowl, combine fried onions, 2 c. breadcrumbs, grated cheese, 4 eggs, and spices and mix well. Form into small logs approximately 3 inches in length. Prepare 2 plates, one containing the remaining 1 c. breadcrumbs and the other the remaining egg (lightly beaten). Dip logs into egg and then breadcrumbs, and place onto a greased 9x13-inch pan. Spray tops of croquettes with oil spray and bake uncovered at 350° for 40 to 45 minutes or until golden on top. Serve alone or accompanied with marinara sauce or sour cream.

Parmesan Tomato Spaghetti With Fried Onions

YOU WILL NEED

3 med. onions, diced

Oil, for frying

1 lb. spaghetti, cooked al dente

1 (4-oz.) can tomato paste

¼ c. olive oil

Salt and pepper, to taste

Grated Parmesan cheese (opt.)

START COOKING

In a frying pan over medium-high heat, fry onions in oil until golden brown and crisp. In a large bowl, combine fried onions, spaghetti, tomato paste, olive oil, salt, and pepper and mix very well. Sprinkle Parmesan cheese over spaghetti before serving.

With few ingredients, this dish is completed in a flash. So tasty and delicious, it will be eaten just as fast!

Omit Parmesan cheese to keep it pareve.

Rice & Vegetable Herb Gratin

YOU WILL NEED

2 T. butter or margarine

1 red onion, diced

2 garlic cloves, minced

1 zucchini, sliced

1 can of whole baby corn, cut in half lengthwise

6 frozen mixed herbs cubes, defrosted (or mix your own choice of fresh herbs to make 3 T.)

½ c. rice, cooked

½ c. grated mozzarella cheese

2 T. breadcrumbs

START COOKING

In a large skillet over medium/high heat, melt butter or margarine. Add onion and sauté, approximately 5 minutes. Add garlic, zucchini, and baby corn and cook for 5 minutes, stirring constantly. Add mixed herbs and rice and mix well to combine. Add half the cheese and season to taste with salt and pepper. Pour mixture into a greased oven dish, sprinkle breadcrumbs evenly over the top, and add remaining grated cheese over the breadcrumbs. Bake at 350° for 40 minutes covered and 15 minutes uncovered, until cheese begins to turn golden.

If you like the flavor of curry, use basmati rice and spice with curry spices!

Warm, Creamy, Cheese and Cauliflower Side Dish

A fantastically rich side — a perfect complement to any fish main dish. This "cheesy" sauce is excellent on other vegetables, too — try using it on broccoli as a variation!

YOU WILL NEED

1 (16-oz.) bag frozen cauliflower, defrosted

3 T. melted butter

¾ tsp. dry mustard

1 tsp. salt

¼ tsp. pepper

1 c. milk

¾ c. mayonnaise

8 oz. shredded mozzarella cheese

½ c. onion, chopped

START COOKING

Place cauliflower in an 8-inch ovenproof casserole dish. Mix butter, mustard, salt, pepper, and milk in a small saucepan over medium-high heat. Bring to a boil and simmer for 1 minute. Remove from heat. Add mayonnaise and cheese, stir until melted. Add onion and mix well. Pour mixture over cauliflower and bake uncovered at 350° for 50–60 minutes.

Corn Fritters

YOU WILL NEED

6 eggs

¾ c. milk

3 c. Homemade Pancake Mix — see p. 119

Salt and pepper, to taste

3 (11-oz.) cans corn niblets, drained

Oil, for frying

Parsley, to garnish (opt.)

START COOKING

In a large bowl, mix eggs, milk, pancake mix, and seasonings with a metal fork. Add corn and mix once again. In a large pan over medium/high heat, heat oil until hot but not smoking. Drop tablespoons of batter into the sizzling oil and fry approximately 2 minutes on each side or until golden. Remove from pan with a slotted spoon and drain on paper towels. Serve on a large platter, garnished with parsley.

These crunchy, crispy fritters are enjoyed by children and adults alike! They will be polished off in seconds!

In Pan Zucchini Kugel

10–12 SERVES
(ONE 9x13 PAN)

DAIRY OR **PAREVE**

YOU WILL NEED

1 c. Homemade Pancake Mix — see p. 119

½ c. grated Parmesan cheese

½ tsp. salt

½ c. oil

Dash of pepper

1 garlic clove, minced

4 eggs, slightly beaten

2 med. zucchini, thinly sliced – do not peel!

1 sm. onion, chopped

START COOKING

In a greased 9x13-inch pan, combine pancake mix, Parmesan cheese, salt, oil, pepper, garlic, and eggs and mix well (it will be slightly lumpy – that's fine). Add zucchini and chopped onion and mix once again. Bake uncovered at 350° for 30–40 minutes or until golden brown. Tip – double recipe if you want a "higher" kugel.

This is an awesome kugel that presents beautifully with virtually no effort! You can keep it pareve by omitting the cheese! Try it — you will not be disappointed!

Fluffy Pancakes

YOU WILL NEED

1 c. Homemade Pancake Mix —
  see p. 119

1 c. milk

1 egg

2 T. sugar (or more if you like your
  pancakes sweeter)

Oil, for frying

START COOKING

In a medium-size bowl, using a metal fork, mix pancake mix, milk, egg, and
sugar until a smooth batter forms. Heat oil in a large skillet over medium/high
heat. Pour batter to desired pancake size and fry for approximately 30–40
seconds on each side. Serve warm with topping of your choice.

Easy Cheese Risotto

YOU WILL NEED

Oil, for frying

1 onion, diced

1½ c. risotto rice

½ c. dry white wine (opt.)

5 c. hot chicken or vegetable stock
  (pareve)

2 T. olive oil

¾ c. grated Parmesan cheese
  (plus a little extra for topping)

Salt and pepper, to taste

START COOKING

Heat oil in a large pot over medium/high heat. Add onion and cook for 2 minutes
or until just starting to soften. Add rice and cook, stirring for 2 more minutes or
until rice is translucent. Carefully pour in the wine (it will bubble and evaporate
almost immediately). Add stock a ladleful at a time, stirring constantly until the
stock is completely absorbed after each addition. This should take approximately
20–25 minutes. The risotto should have a creamy consistency, and the rice
should be tender but have a little bite. Remove pot from heat. Stir in olive oil and
Parmesan cheese and season to taste with the salt and pepper. Cover and let sit
for 1 minute. Serve topped with Parmesan cheese.

4-6 SERVES

DAIRY

Three Cheese Leek and Potato Layer Bake

YOU WILL NEED

4 lg. potatoes, peeled

1 leek, sliced (white part only)

3–4 garlic cloves, minced

½ c. grated cheddar cheese

1¾ c. grated mozzarella cheese

¼ c. grated Parmesan cheese

4 parsley cubes, defrosted

Salt and pepper, to taste

⅔ c. heavy cream

⅔ c. milk

START COOKING

In a medium-size pan, boil potatoes in lightly salted boiling water for 15 minutes. Drain and allow to cool. Cut potatoes into thin slices and place a layer at the bottom of a greased ovenproof dish. Layer as follows: leek, garlic, cheeses, and parsley, and season well with salt and pepper. Repeat layers, ending with a layer of cheese. In a small bowl, combine cream, milk, salt and pepper and pour over the layers. Bake uncovered at 350° for 1 ¼ hours or until cheese is golden brown and bubbling, and the potatoes are tender.

Cheesy Baked Tomato Rice

YOU WILL NEED

2 T. oil

1 onion, diced

1 red pepper, diced

2 garlic cloves, minced

1½ c. long grain rice

4 c. vegetable stock (4 tsp. vegetable or pareve
  chicken soup mix, dissolved in 4 c. boiling water)

2 (8-oz.) cans of chopped tomatoes

4 frozen basil cubes

1½ c. grated cheddar cheese

3 T. grated Parmesan cheese

*A perfect side dish for your
dairy meal!*

START COOKING

Heat oil in a large skillet over medium-high heat. Add onion and red pepper
and cook, stirring frequently for 5 minutes or until soft. Add garlic and cook for
another 2 minutes. Add rice and continue to stir often, until rice is translucent.
Stir in stock and tomatoes and bring to a boil. Lower heat and simmer for 5
minutes or until stock is almost completely absorbed. Stir in basil and cheeses
and pour into a greased 9x13-inch pan. Bake tightly covered at 350° for 25
minutes.

Broccoli Cheese Casserole

YOU WILL NEED

2 oz. butter

2 T. flour

1 tsp. salt

½ c. water

8 oz. grated mozzarella cheese

4 eggs, beaten

1 c. cracker crumbs (Snackers or Tam-Tams)

2 (24-oz.) pkgs. frozen chopped broccoli florets, defrosted

START COOKING

In a medium-size pot over medium/high heat, melt butter. Add flour, salt, and water. Stir until smooth. Add grated cheese and eggs, stirring until thick. In a small bowl, combine half of cracker crumbs together with broccoli. Add sauce over broccoli and mix to combine. Pour into a 9x13 ovenproof casserole dish and sprinkle remaining cracker crumbs on top. Bake uncovered at 350° for 45 minutes.

Mini Bite-Size Quiches

YOU WILL NEED

½ c. red green pepper, chopped

¼ c. scallions, chopped

Oil, for sautéing

2 eggs

2 egg whites

1 tsp. chili powder (opt.)

⅛ tsp. pepper

½ tsp. salt

½ c. shredded cheddar cheese

START COOKING

In a small skillet, sauté pepper and scallions until tender, approximately 5 minutes. In a small bowl, beat eggs slightly with a metal fork. Add cheese and spices and mix thoroughly to combine. Add sautéed vegetables and mix well. Spoon 1 T. mixture into each greased mini muffin pan section. Bake at 350° for 15–20 minutes or until centers are set. Cool a little before removing from pan. Serve hot or warm.

This is a moist garlic bread that comes out perfect every time! An excellent accompaniment to any soup or addition to your dairy meal!

Parmesan Garlic Bread

YOU WILL NEED

2 T. unsalted butter, softened

2 T. extra virgin olive oil

2 tsp. finely chopped garlic
(or 2 garlic cubes)

2 T. fresh chopped parsley
(or 2 parsley cubes)

1 (15x3.5) French loaf
(you can also use baguettes)

¼ c. grated Parmesan cheese

START COOKING

In a small bowl, combine butter, oil, garlic and parsley. Cut the bread into 1-inch-thick slices without cutting completely through, leaving the slices still attached to each other. As you gently pull apart the slices, brush the garlic mixture onto each slice and sprinkle with Parmesan cheese. Wrap the loaf in aluminum foil and bake in the middle of the oven for 15 minutes. Open the aluminum foil and bake uncovered for another 5 minutes.

Cauliflower and Potato Bake

YOU WILL NEED

1 (16-oz.) pkg. cauliflower florets (defrost if using frozen)

2 lg. potatoes, peeled and cubed

Sauce:

2 T. butter or margarine

1 leek, sliced (white part only)

1 garlic clove, minced

2 T. flour

1¼ c. milk

¾ c. grated cheese of your choice

½ tsp. pepper

4 frozen parsley cubes, defrosted

Salt and pepper, to taste

START COOKING

Cook cauliflower and potatoes in a pot of boiling water for 10 minutes. Drain well and set aside in an ovenproof dish. In a medium-size pot, melt butter or margarine over medium/high heat. Add leek and garlic and sauté for 1–2 minutes. Add flour and mix well. Remove from heat and slowly stir in milk, ½ c. cheese, pepper, and parsley and mix well. Return pot to the fire and bring to a boil, stirring continuously. Season with salt and pepper. Pour over cauliflower and potato and sprinkle the remaining ¼ c. cheese evenly on top. Bake uncovered at 350° for 30–40 minutes, or until vegetables are tender and cheese is golden brown. To prepare this dish ahead of time, have it prepared until ready to bake. Bake approximately half an hour before you plan to serve.

Roasted Parmesan Asparagus

YOU WILL NEED

2 bunches of fresh asparagus

6 T. olive oil

4 T. grated Parmesan cheese

4 T. garlic powder

1 T. salt

START COOKING

In a small bowl combine olive oil, Parmesan cheese, garlic powder, and salt.
Place asparagus onto a well-greased cookie sheet and pour oil mixture over
the asparagus, making sure they are well coated. Bake uncovered at 350° for
30–40 minutes or until desired tenderness.

*A super easy but elegant
side dish!*

Pierogi Lasagna

YOU WILL NEED

12 lasagna noodles

⅓ c. vegetable oil

5 sm. onions, finely chopped (approximately 3 c.)

¼ tsp. salt

½ tsp. black pepper

1½ c. shredded cheddar cheese

½ c. shredded cheddar cheese for topping

6 c. warm mashed potatoes, instant or homemade

START COOKING

Cook lasagna noodles according to package directions, drain, and set aside. In a large skillet over medium/high heat, heat oil until hot but not smoking. Add approximately 2½ cups chopped onions and salt, and sauté for 10–15 minutes, or until lightly browned. Reserve ½ cup sautéed onions for topping. Place 3 to 4 lasagna noodles at the bottom of a greased 9x13-inch pan. Spread a third of the potato mixture over the noodles. Sprinkle sautéed onions over the potato mixture. Repeat layers until a total of 4 layers of noodles and 3 layers of potato mixture have been placed, with a layer of noodles on top. Top with remaining sautéed onions and cheese. Cover with aluminum foil and bake at 350° for 25–30 minutes or until heated through.

Variation: Add a layer of marinara sauce in between the noodles and potatoes or add fresh mushrooms together with the onions!

SERVES 10–12

(ONE 9x13 PAN)

DAIRY

An excellent side dish with everyone's favorite ingredients!

DAIRY

A delicious twist to your standard macaroni and cheese! If serving as a side dish, serve in individual ramekins on a platter.

Winter Squash Mac and Cheese

YOU WILL NEED

1 (16-oz.) box elbow macaroni

1 T. salt

2 T. butter

2 T. flour

½ tsp. powdered mustard

2 c. milk

1 c. grated cheddar cheese

1 c. grated mozzarella cheese

Salt and pepper, to taste

1 (12-oz.) box frozen winter squash, defrosted

Topping:

½ c. breadcrumbs

½ c. grated cheese of your choice

START COOKING

Bring a large pot of water to a boil over high heat. Add 1 T. salt and the pasta; cook until pasta is tender. Drain and return the pasta to the pot. In a medium-size saucepan, melt the butter over medium/high heat. Once the foaming has subsided, add the flour and mustard. Whisk vigorously for 1 minute. Gradually whisk in the milk a little at a time, mixing continuously. Bring the mixture to a simmer over medium heat and continue to mix. Lower heat to medium-low and continue to simmer for another 5–6 minutes, until the mixture has the consistency of heavy cream. Add the cheeses, salt, pepper, and squash, stirring until the cheese melts. Pour the sauce over the drained pasta and stir thoroughly. Pour pasta into a greased 9x13-inch dish. Sprinkle with breadcrumbs and ½ c. cheese and bake at 350° for 40 minutes or until golden on top.

Parmesan Zucchini Sticks

4 SERVES

DAIRY

YOU WILL NEED

2 med. zucchini, unpeeled

2 eggs, lightly beaten

1½ c. plain breadcrumbs

½ c. grated Parmesan cheese

1 c. flour

4 T. olive oil

Salt and pepper, to taste

To serve: marinara sauce

START COOKING

Cut the zucchini into 1-inch sticks and set aside. Prepare 3 plates; one with flour, a second plate with the eggs, seasoned generously with salt and pepper, and a third with the breadcrumbs and parmesan cheese combined. Place a large skillet over medium/high heat and heat the oil until hot but not smoking. Dip each zucchini stick into the flour, eggs, and breadcrumbs and place into the hot oil. Fry the zucchini sticks on both sides, and then drain on paper towels. Serve with marinara sauce.

Mains
&
Meat

SERVES 6

MEAT

This dish is delicious and gets so many compliments each and every time!

Whole Pieces Sesame Chicken

YOU WILL NEED

6 chicken bottoms

1 c. breadcrumbs

1 T. apricot jelly

½ c. ketchup

¾ c. brown sugar

½ c. water

¼ c. sesame seeds

START COOKING

Place breadcrumbs in a bag. Moisten chicken with water and shake in bag with breadcrumbs. Place chicken in a greased 9x13-inch pan; bake covered at 350° for 30 minutes. Mix jelly, ketchup, brown sugar, and water in a small pot and bring to a boil. Remove from heat and pour sauce over chicken. Sprinkle sesame seeds over chicken and bake uncovered for another 45 minutes.

Spicy Chicken

YOU WILL NEED

6 chicken bottoms

Sauce:

1 T. Frank's hot sauce

2 T. ketchup

½ c. apricot jelly

½ c. hot and spicy duck sauce

2 T. onion soup mix

If you like your chicken with a little zing, this recipe is for you!

START COOKING

Combine all sauce ingredients in a bowl and mix well. Place chicken in a greased 9x13-inch pan. Spread sauce evenly over chicken and bake at 350° for 1½ hours covered and ½ hour uncovered.

Honey and Sweet Potato Chicken

Perfect for Rosh Hashanah!

YOU WILL NEED

6–8 chicken bottoms

4 lg. sweet potatoes, cut into chunks

1 lg. onion, sliced

1 c. honey

START COOKING

Place ⅓ of the onion slices at the bottom of a large pot. Put 2–3 chicken pieces on top of onions. Drizzle ⅓ of the honey over chicken. Layer ⅓ of onions on top. Scatter sweet potatoes over onions. Continue in this order, ending with sweet potatoes. Cook on a very low flame for 3½ hours.

Zesty Chicken

YOU WILL NEED

1 whole chicken (quartered) or 6 chicken bottoms

Salt, pepper and paprika, to taste

2 garlic cloves, minced

½ c. duck sauce

½ c. French dressing

1 sm. onion, diced

3 carrots

3 potatoes (reg. or sweet)

1 (10-oz.) box mushrooms (opt.)

START COOKING

Place chicken in a greased 9x13 pan. Sprinkle with spices and minced garlic. Pour duck sauce and French dressing evenly over the chicken. Surround the chicken with the vegetables. Bake uncovered at 350° for 1½ hours.

Easy and Delicious Chicken

YOU WILL NEED

1 chicken, cut into eighths, or 4 chicken bottoms

Sauce:

1 c. apricot jelly

¼ c. mayonnaise

2 T. onion soup mix

START COOKING

Place chicken in a 9x13-inch pan. Mix all sauce ingredients together until thoroughly combined. Pour sauce over chicken. Bake covered at 350° for 1 hour. Uncover and continue to cook for another hour, basting every 20 minutes.

Crispy Honey Lemon Chicken

YOU WILL NEED

4 chicken bottoms

2 eggs, beaten

1 c. breadcrumbs

6 T. honey

4–5 T. lemon juice

A little hot water

START COOKING

Place eggs and breadcrumbs on 2 separate plates. Dip each chicken piece into eggs and then breadcrumbs. Place in a greased 9x13 pan, bottom side up. Bake covered at 350° for 40 minutes. In a small bowl, combine honey, lemon juice, and a little hot water to make a smooth liquid mixture. After 40 minutes, remove chicken from oven and turn over. Drizzle honey/lemon mixture over chicken and return to oven for at least 1 more hour uncovered.

4-6 SERVES

MEAT

Continental Honey Chicken

YOU WILL NEED

1 whole chicken (either whole or quartered)

Sauce:

¾ c. honey

¼ c. ketchup

2 T. mustard

START COOKING

Place chicken in a 9x13-inch pan. Mix all sauce ingredients together in a small bowl. Pour over chicken and bake uncovered at 350° for 2 hours.

Orange Glazed Chicken

4 SERVES

MEAT

Tangy and divine!

YOU WILL NEED

4 chicken bottoms, skin removed

1 c. orange juice

3 T. brown sugar

3 T. soy sauce

3 garlic cloves, minced

¾ c. water

2 T. cornstarch

Salt and pepper, to taste

START COOKING

Place chicken in a 9x13-inch pan. Combine all sauce ingredients and pour over chicken. Bake covered at 350° for 1½ hours.

Hawaiian Chicken

A tropical twist to your chicken!

YOU WILL NEED

6 chicken bottoms
½ c. all-purpose flour
1 tsp. paprika
2 T. garlic powder

Sauce:

1 (24-oz.) can pineapple chunks
   with syrup
1 T. soy sauce
½ c. sugar
½ tsp. salt
1 T. ketchup

START COOKING

Place chicken in a 9x13-inch pan. Mix all sauce ingredients together in a small bowl. Pour over chicken and bake uncovered at 350° for 2 hours.

Italian Chicken

YOU WILL NEED

6–8 chicken bottoms with skin
1 yellow squash, unpeeled
1 green zucchini, unpeeled

1 qt. cherry tomatoes, halved
1 (8-oz.) bottle Italian dressing

START COOKING

Preheat oven to 350°. Place chicken in 9x13-inch pan. Slice squash and zucchini into moons and scatter over chicken. Add tomatoes. Drizzle dressing over chicken and bake uncovered for 2 hours. Remove chicken to a platter. Toss vegetables in the liquid of the pan and then scatter over the chicken.

Tri-Color Pepper Chicken Cutlets

YOU WILL NEED

4–6 chicken cutlets

2 eggs, beaten

½ c. flour

1 onion, diced

3 different colored peppers, cut into strips

12 oz. apricot jam

2 T. brown sugar

¾ c. ketchup

The sauce bursts with flavor and color in this tasty dish!

START COOKING

Prepare egg and flour in 2 separate plates. Dip chicken into egg and then flour and place in a greased 9x13-inch pan. Sauté onion and peppers, until onions are translucent and peppers are soft. In a small bowl, combine apricot jam, brown sugar, and ketchup. Pour over chicken and place sautéed vegetables on top. Bake at 350° for 1½ hours covered and 30 minutes uncovered.

Kishke Chicken

YOU WILL NEED

6 chicken bottoms with skin
Salt and pepper, to season
2 celery stalks, finely diced
2 carrots, finely diced
1 onion, finely diced

1 tsp. salt
¾ T. paprika
½ c. oil
1½ c. flour
½ c. honey

START COOKING

Season chicken with salt and pepper. Combine celery, carrots, onion, salt, paprika, oil, and flour and mix well. Stuff each piece of chicken with a small amount of the mixture under the skin. Bake covered at 350° for 2 hours. Baste with honey and bake uncovered for another 15 minutes. (Stuffing can be prepared in advance and frozen.)

Heavenly Chicken and Potatoes

YOU WILL NEED

6 chicken bottoms
1 pkg. onion soup mix
1 c. Russian or Thousand Island
    dressing

1 (12-oz.) jar apricot jam
3 lbs. Idaho potatoes, peeled and
    sliced

START COOKING

In a medium-size bowl, combine soup mix, dressing, and apricot jam and mix well. Place potato slices on the bottom of a greased 9x13-inch pan. Place chicken on top and pour sauce over chicken. Bake covered at 350° for at least 2 hours or until potatoes are done.

*A meal in a pan!
Serve chicken and potatoes
on separate platters.
No one will know they were
cooked together!*

Spicy Citrus Chicken

YOU WILL NEED

6 chicken bottoms or breasts
    on the bone
2 T. olive oil
4 T. lime or lemon juice
2 T. orange juice
2 T. paprika

1 tsp. chili powder (opt.)
½–1 tsp. cayenne pepper (depending
    on how hot you like it)
½ tsp. pepper
½ tsp. salt

START COOKING

Place all ingredients except chicken into a large baking dish; add chicken and flip over several times to coat. Bake uncovered at 350° for 1¼ hours.

Sticky Chicken

YOU WILL NEED

6 chicken bottoms
2 T. oil
1 T. soy sauce

3 T. smooth peanut butter
3 T. ketchup

START COOKING

In a small bowl, whisk together with a fork: oil, soy sauce, peanut butter, and ketchup. Place chicken in a 9x13-inch pan; pour mixture over chicken. Turn chicken over and then back again in order to coat. Bake uncovered at 350° for 1¼ hours, basting several times.

Batter Dipped Chicken with a Choice of Two Sauces

YOU WILL NEED

6 chicken cutlets, cut into cubes

Batter:

2 eggs

½ c. pareve milk (soy, rice dream, or coffee creamer)

2 T. sugar

1 c. flour

½ tsp. baking powder

Oil, for frying

SERVES 6

MEAT

Not a bit of this will be left over! This dish is as popular with kids as with adults! Try serving this right away as reheating takes away a little of the crunch!

START COOKING

In a medium-size mixing bowl, combine all batter ingredients, beating vigorously with a fork until smooth. Heat at least 1 inch of oil in a frying pan until hot but not smoking. Lower heat to medium flame. Dip chicken cubes into batter and immediately drop into hot oil; fry until golden brown. (You may have to do this in batches.)

Sauce for Sweet and Sour Chicken:

¾ c. sugar

⅓ c. ketchup

1 T. soy sauce

¾ c. water

2 T. lemon juice

3 T. cornstarch

½ (20-oz.) can pineapple chunks with ½ of the juice

In a small pot, boil sugar, ketchup, soy sauce, half of the water, and lemon juice. Combine cornstarch and remaining water in a cup and add it to the pot, mixing vigorously as you bring it to a boil again. Add pineapple chunks with juice and serve warm as a dipping sauce, or pour over chicken pieces just before serving.

Sauce for Lemon Chicken:

½ c. sugar

1 c. boiling water

2 T. lemon juice

¼ tsp. salt

1 T. margarine

1 T. cornstarch dissolved in 1 T. water

In a small pot over medium/high heat, combine sugar, water, lemon juice, salt, and margarine. Mix well and bring to a boil. Lower heat. Slowly add cornstarch mixture, stirring vigorously until sauce thickens. Remove from heat. Serve warm as a dipping sauce or pour over chicken pieces just before serving.

Mushroom Garlic Chicken Marsala

SERVES 6

MEAT

YOU WILL NEED

6 thin chicken cutlets

½ c. flour

1 tsp. garlic powder

1 tsp. onion powder

Oil, for searing

1 (15-oz.) can mushrooms

2 lg. onions, diced

2 garlic cloves, minced

¼ c. light wine (low alcohol)

3 T. mushroom soup mix

3 T. flour

¾ c. water

START COOKING

Rinse chicken cutlets; do not dry. On a flat plate, combine flour, garlic powder, and onion powder. Dip both sides of chicken into flour mixture to coat evenly. Heat oil in a large skillet over medium/high heat. Sear chicken for 2 minutes on each side. Remove chicken from skillet and place in a 9x13-inch pan. In the same skillet, sauté onion and garlic until translucent, approximately 5 minutes. Add mushrooms and soup mix and sauté for 2–3 minutes more, then add flour and mix well. Slowly add wine and water a little at a time, while stirring continuously to ensure that no lumps are formed. Pour mixture over chicken; bake covered at 350° for 30 minutes.

You can freeze this dish before baking and bake straight from the freezer for 1 hour and 20 minutes. Chicken is soft and silky!

Marinated Chicken Kebabs

What an awesome dish! Serve a platter of these chicken skewers as a main course or 1–2 on a bed of rice as a starter!

YOU WILL NEED

6 chicken cutlets, cut into ½-inch cubes
½ c. apricot jam
2 T. soy sauce
½ c. ketchup
¼ c. brown sugar

1 T. garlic powder
2 T. mustard
Vegetables of your choice (peppers, onions, mushrooms), cut into ½-inch cubes

START COOKING

In a medium bowl, combine jam, soy sauce, ketchup, brown sugar, garlic powder, and mustard, using a fork to mix well. Pour marinade together with chicken cubes into a Ziploc bag. Refrigerate for 3 hours or overnight. Remove chicken from refrigerator and, alternating with vegetable cubes, arrange on skewers. Place skewers in a large roasting pan. Bake at 350° for 20 minutes. Turn skewers over and bake for another 10 minutes or until chicken is cooked through.

Asian Orange Chicken

YOU WILL NEED

4 boneless skinless chicken breasts, cut into cubes

2 c. flour

½ tsp. salt

½ tsp. pepper

3 T. olive oil

Sauce:

3 c. water

½ c. orange juice

½ c. lemon juice

⅔ c. rice vinegar

2 tsp. sesame oil

3 T. soy sauce

2 c. brown sugar

2 garlic cloves, minced

4 T. (or 1 bunch) chopped scallions

½ tsp. red pepper flakes

2 T. cornstarch dissloved in 2 T. water

Scrumptious! Tastes like you bought it at a takeout! Serve with basmati rice.

START COOKING

In a medium pot over high heat, combine water, juices, rice vinegar, sesame oil, and soy sauce. Add sugar, garlic, scallions, and red pepper flakes and bring to a boil. Lower heat. Slowly add cornstarch mixture to sauce, stirring continuously until thickened. Place chicken in a Ziploc bag with 1 c. sauce. If you have time, refrigerate for 2 hours. In another Ziploc bag, mix flour, salt, and pepper. Add chicken cubes, seal, shake, and coat evenly. Heat oil in a large skillet over medium heat and pan fry chicken until brown on both sides. Set aside. Wipe out skillet, add sauce, and bring to a boil. Lower heat and add chicken. Simmer for 5–10 minutes, stirring occasionally.

Sesame Honey Roasted Cornish Hens

The glaze gives it a deep brown caramel color — looks and tastes professional!

YOU WILL NEED

4 Cornish hens

Glaze:

2 T. sesame oil

½ c. soy sauce

½ c. honey

4 T. lemon juice

2 T. sesame seeds

START COOKING

In a small pot over medium heat, place all glaze ingredients and cook, stirring continuously for 10 minutes. In a large roasting pan, place Cornish hens, breast side up, and pour glaze evenly over them. Bake uncovered, basting several times, at 350° for 2 hours.

SERVES 6

MEAT

Savory Chinese Chicken

YOU WILL NEED

2 lbs. chicken cutlets, cut into long strips

¾ c. soy sauce

1 red pepper, sliced into long strips

1 green pepper, sliced into long strips

5 scallions, sliced

4 T. cornstarch

1 c. water

START COOKING

In a Ziploc bag, marinate chicken strips in soy sauce for 2 hours in refrigerator. In a medium skillet, sauté peppers and scallions for 5–10 minutes. Add chicken and marinade. Dissolve corn starch in water and add to mixture. Boil until thick. Simmer for 30–40 minutes or until chicken is no longer pink in the middle.

Honey Apricot Chicken Kebabs

YOU WILL NEED

4 boneless skinless chicken breasts, cut into ½-inch cubes
2 T. margarine
1 T. honey
3 T. lemon juice
2 tsp. apricot jam
1/8 tsp. black pepper
2 red peppers, cut into ½-inch chunks
To serve: cooked rice

Who would think you could cook kebabs on a stove top?!

START COOKING

Melt margarine in a large frying pan over medium heat. Add honey, lemon juice, apricot jam, and black pepper. Stir for 2–3 minutes or until honey and jam have melted and mixture is combined well. Thread chicken and red pepper cubes, alternately, onto 8 lightly oiled wooden skewers. Place skewers into pan and, turning frequently, cook for 20 minutes or until chicken is cooked through. Remove skewers from pan and reserve sauce. Serve skewers over a bed of rice with sauce spooned over entire platter.

Whole Roasted Chicken

YOU WILL NEED

1 whole chicken

½ lemon

10 whole garlic cloves

Salt and pepper, to sprinkle inside cavity

⅛ tsp. pepper and ½ tsp. salt, combined

3 lb. sm. red potatoes

1 stick margarine, melted

START COOKING

Place chicken into a large roasting pan. Place lemon and 5 garlic cloves into the cavity of chicken and sprinkle salt and pepper inside. Then rub salt and pepper combination over chicken. Arrange potatoes around chicken and scatter remaining 5 garlic cloves among the potatoes. Drizzle margarine over chicken and potatoes and bake chicken uncovered at 350° for 40 minutes. Baste and continue to cook for another hour, basting every 20 minutes.

A simple roast chicken that comes out soft and succulent every time!

Honey Almond Chicken and Rice

YOU WILL NEED

1 lb. cutlets, cut into cubes

1 (6-oz.) pkg. rice pilaf

¼ c. honey

¼ c. orange juice

3 T. soy sauce

1 garlic clove, minced

1 T. cornstarch

1 T. oil

2 c. snow peas

⅓ c. sliced almonds

To serve: cooked rice

START COOKING

Prepare rice pilaf according to package directions; set aside. Mix honey, orange juice, soy sauce, garlic, and ginger together in a small pot over medium heat. Add cornstarch and mix well until sauce begins to thicken. Heat oil in skillet and cook chicken for 5–8 minutes. Add sauce, snow peas, and almonds and cook for 10 more minutes. Serve over rice.

SERVES 10–12

MEAT

Awesome and way healthier than deli roll!

Meat and Chicken Roll

YOU WILL NEED

1 puff pastry dough

Mixture 1:

1 lb. chopped meat

1 egg

½ c. breadcrumbs

1 tsp. garlic powder

½ tsp. salt

½ tsp. pepper

Mixture 2:

1 lb. chopped chicken

1 egg

1 tsp. garlic powder

½ c. breadcrumbs

½ tsp. salt

⅛ tsp. pepper

To spread:

1 sm. can tomato sauce

4 T. brown sugar

⅛ tsp. salt

⅛ tsp. pepper

Egg, for brushing

Sesame seeds

START COOKING

Place ingredients of each meat mixture in a separate bowl and mix well. In a small bowl, combine tomato sauce, brown sugar, salt, and pepper. Unroll puff pastry dough and spread tomato sauce mixture evenly over dough until the edges. Spread chicken mixture over tomato sauce mixture — it is fine if there are gaps! Spread meat mixture over chicken mixture and roll up jelly-roll style. Brush roll with egg and sprinkle on top with sesame seeds. Bake uncovered at 350° for 1¼ hours.

Crockpot Pastrami Roast

YOU WILL NEED

3–4 lb. pastrami roast

¾ c. brown sugar

¼ c. honey

2 T. mustard

Water

START COOKING

Place pastrami roast in crockpot and fill with water halfway up the roast. In a small bowl, combine rest of ingredients and pour over meat. Cook on low for 8 hours or overnight.

An amazing dish especially for a Yom Tov with a Shabbos connected to it, as you already have the crockpot on!

Minute Steaks

YOU WILL NEED

6 minute steaks
Pinch of salt and pepper
Garlic powder
Onion powder
1 lg. onion, sliced
¼ c. ketchup
2–3 T. honey
1 T. vinegar
1 T. water

START COOKING

Season meat with salt, pepper, garlic powder, and onion powder. Place sliced onions on the bottom of a 9x13-inch pan and put meat on top. Mix ketchup, honey, vinegar, and water and pour over meat. Bake covered at 350° for at least 2 hours.

Soft and tender!

Tongue

YOU WILL NEED

4–5 lb. pickled beef tongue
½ c. brown sugar
½–¾ c. ketchup
¼ c. water

START COOKING

Boil tongue for 2 hours. Let cool and peel. Cube into bite-size pieces. Mix rest of ingredients together and place in pot with tongue pieces. Simmer on low for 30 minutes or until tongue is soft.

Beware — there is never a slice left of this meat!

SERVES 8

MEAT

This is an impressive dish — perfect l'kavod Yom Tov!

Standing Rib Roast

YOU WILL NEED

4 lb. roast (French roast or brisket)
3 lg. onions, sliced
4 whole garlic cloves
2 celery stalks, chopped
2 tsp. black pepper

3 T. vinegar
2 T. olive oil
¼ c. honey
1 (750-ml) bottle dry red wine
   (approx. 25 oz.)

START COOKING

Place onions, garlic, and celery on the bottom of a large roasting pan. Place meat on top. Sprinkle meat with black pepper and then pour vinegar, olive oil, and honey onto the meat. Add red wine. Cover and marinate for at least 1 hour. Making sure roasting pan is tightly covered, bake at 350° for 4 hours (if the meat has a bone, bake for 6 hours). Cool completely before slicing.

APPROX 6 SERVES

MEAT

Due to the roasting in a bag, this meat comes out so tender. It will amaze you!

Roast Beef in a Roasting Bag

YOU WILL NEED

2½ lb. roast (French roast or brisket)

Sauce:
1 T. oil
2 lg. onions, diced
3 garlic cloves, minced

¼ c. lemon juice
½ c. water
¾ c. brown sugar
½ c. ketchup
1 T. flour

START COOKING

In a medium-size skillet, sauté onions and garlic until translucent, approximately 5 minutes. Add lemon juice, water, brown sugar, ketchup, and flour and mix well to combine. Place a roasting bag in a pan and put the roast in the bag. Pour in the sauce and close the bag according to oven bag directions. Bake at 350° for 3 hours.

Pepper Steak

YOU WILL NEED

2 lbs. pepper steak

¼ c. oil

3 T. onion soup mix

1 c. boiling water

2 tsp. sugar

1 T. soy sauce

1 green pepper, diced

1 onion, diced

1 tomato, diced

Mushrooms (opt.)

2 T. cornstarch

START COOKING

Heat oil in skillet and cook pepper steak until browned. Combine soup mix, water, sugar, and soy sauce. Pour over meat and bring to a boil. Add vegetables to meat and continue to simmer, covered, for approximately 2 more hours. Add cornstarch, whisking briskly until sauce has thickened. Serve warm.

By far the best recipe for pepper steak!

Sweet and Sour French Roast

YOU WILL NEED

4 lb. French roast

Sauce:

½ c. ketchup

¼ c. vinegar

½ c. brown sugar

1. c. fried onions

START COOKING

In a medium-size bowl, combine ketchup, vinegar, and brown sugar to make a smooth paste. Add onions and mix until thoroughly combined. Place roast in a 9x13-inch pan and pour sauce over meat. Cover with 2 or 3 pieces of aluminum foil and bake at 350° for 2 hours for medium rare or 3 hours for well done.

If you have a variety of preferences from your family members when it comes to cooking meat, cook it medium rare and serve the end slices for the people who like it more well done!

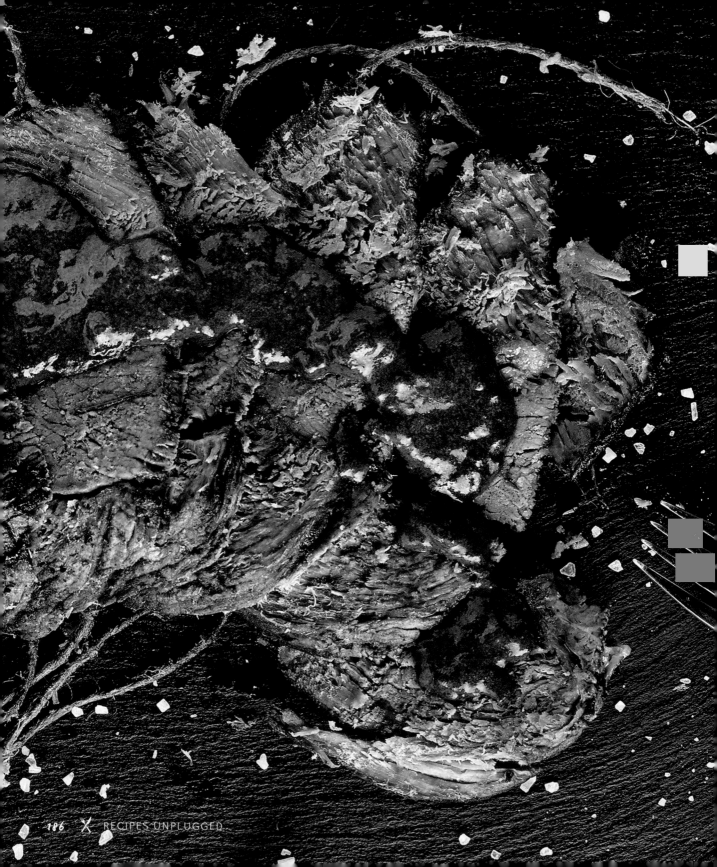

Soft Stove Top Roast Bee

YOU WILL NEED

3–4lb. French roast or brisket

1 lg. onion, diced

2 T. oil

1 (4-oz.) can tomato sauce

1 T. salt

⅛ tsp. pepper

1 tsp. paprika

1 garlic clove, minced

¾–1 c. red wine

START COOKING

In a large skillet, sauté onion in oil until translucent, approximately 5 minutes. Add tomato sauce, salt, pepper, paprika, and garlic and mix well. Place roast in a pot and pour wine over meat. Cover and cook on low flame for 1½ hours, turning over after 45 minutes. When meat is cool, slice (it will be rare in the middle) and cook for 10 more minutes in the gravy.

4-6 SERVES

MEAT

Warning! These are literally finger-lickin' good!

Spectacular Spare Ribs

YOU WILL NEED

2 lbs. ribs

1 T. cornstarch

2 T. vinegar

½ c. water

2 T. ketchup

¼ c. soy sauce

⅓ c. brown sugar

START COOKING

Place ribs in a roasting pan and bake covered at 350° for 45 minutes. Remove from oven and carefully pour off fat. In a small pot over medium/high heat, combine rest of ingredients and bring to a boil, stirring constantly. Pour sauce over ribs; bake uncovered for another 2 hours, basting 2 or 3 times.

Broccoli Stuffed Capons

YOU WILL NEED

4–6 sm. capons

½ bag frozen broccoli florets

4 T. mayonnaise

4 T. mustard

4 T. honey

1 (2.8-oz.) can French's onions, crushed by hand

START COOKING

Unroll capons and place 2–3 broccoli florets on top of each one, with heads sticking out at both ends. Roll up neatly and place seam-side down in a greased 9x13-inch pan. In a small bowl, mix mayonnaise, mustard, and honey into a smooth paste and spread on top of capons. Sprinkle French's onions over capons and bake at 350° for 1½ hours covered and 20 minutes uncovered

The beauty of capons is that they hardly ever dry out; this recipe is not only divine but as easy as can be to make!

Pastrami Stuffed Capons

YOU WILL NEED

4–6 capons

Stuffing:

1½ c. flour

½ c. oil

¼ c. sugar

1 tsp. salt

1½ tsp. baking powder

¾ c. boiled water

4 slices pastrami, shredded

Sauce:

1 T. lemon juice

1 tsp. salt

1 tsp. paprika

⅛ tsp. pepper

¾ c. duck sauce

1 sm. can French's onions, crushed by hand

START COOKING

In a medium-size bowl, mix stuffing ingredients until thoroughly combined. Unroll capons. Place approximately 1 heaping tablespoon of stuffing onto each capon. Roll up neatly and place seam-side down in a 9x13-inch pan. Combine all sauce ingredients in a small bowl and pour over capons. Sprinkle French's onions over capons and bake at 350° for 1¾ hours covered and 20 minutes uncovered.

"Delicious" does not do this justice!

Beware — there is never a slice left of this meat!

Glorious Glazed Corned Beef

YOU WILL NEED

3 lb. corned beef, pickled

Glaze:

¾ c. ketchup

2 T. mustard

4 T. oil

2 c. brown sugar

START COOKING

Place corned beef into a large pot of water and bring to a boil. Lower heat and simmer for 2 hours. Remove meat from pot, cool, and slice. Place into a 9x13-inch pan. In a small bowl, combine all glaze ingredients. and pour over corned beef. Bake covered at 350° for 30 minutes.

Turkey Breast on the Bone

YOU WILL NEED

1 lg. turkey breast (or a netted turkey)

1 T. paprika

1 T. garlic powder

1 T. onion powder

½ T. salt

1 tsp. pepper

6 T. oil

2 T. water

START COOKING

Place turkey in roasting pan. Combine rest of ingredients to form a smooth paste. Spread paste over turkey and roast uncovered at 350° for 1½ hours. Remove turkey from bone, slice, and serve.

Turkey Roast

YOU WILL NEED

3–4 lb. turkey roast

1 c. brown sugar

1 c. ketchup

¾ c. water

¼ c. oil

3 T. balsamic vinegar

3 T. soy sauce

1 sm. onion, diced

START COOKING

Place turkey in roasting pan. Combine remaining ingredients and pour over turkey. Bake at 350° for 1½ hours covered and for 30 minutes uncovered.

If you are not a turkey fan, this recipe is for you! It is so tasty that even people who do not eat turkey like this dish!

This soufflé can also be mixed directly in the pan!

This is the only soufflé recipe I know that can be made in advance without having to be served immediately. It will sink a little in the center and the texture will be slightly altered, but it is still equally delicious when reheated!

Super Easy Cheese Soufflé

YOU WILL NEED

8 eggs
¾ c. flour
2 c. milk
2 c. mayonnaise (you can use low-fat)
3 c. shredded cheese
1 tsp. garlic powder
Salt and pepper, to taste

START COOKING

In a large mixing bowl, combine eggs, flour, milk, mayonnaise, cheese, garlic powder, salt, and pepper and mix well (it will be lumpy). Pour into a greased 9x13-inch pan and bake uncovered at 350° for 45—50 minutes or until golden brown on top.

This is an absolutely wonderful dish, definitely worth the extra step of stuffing the shells! It's sure to become a family favorite!

Stuffed Jumbo Shells

YOU WILL NEED

1 (12-oz.) pkg. jumbo shells, cooked according to package directions

2 (8 oz.) pkgs. grated mozzarella cheese

1 lb. farmer cheese

2 eggs

Sauce:

1 (28 oz.) can tomato sauce

1 (28 oz.) can crushed tomatoes

3 tsp. brown sugar

3 tsp. sugar

1 garlic clove, minced

START COOKING

In a medium-size bowl, combine mozzarella cheese, farmer cheese and eggs and mix well. Use approximately 2 tablespoons of the cheese mixture to stuff each shell, placing them in a 9x13 pan when stuffed. In a large mixing bowl, combine all sauce ingredients and mix well. Pour sauce over shells and bake covered at 350° for 1 hour.

Pasta Primavera

10–12
SERVES

DAIRY

YOU WILL NEED

3 c. rotini pasta, uncooked

½ lb. fresh green beans, cut into 2-inch lengths (2 c.)

1 T. butter

1 T. olive oil

1 lb. asparagus (2½ c.)

1 red pepper, thinly sliced and cut into 1½-inch strips

Salt and pepper, to taste

2 T. flour

1½ c. whole milk

1 c. frozen peas

⅓ c. grated Parmesan cheese

⅛ tsp. black pepper

START COOKING

Cook pasta in water according to package directions, adding green beans during the last five minutes. Drain. In a large skillet over medium/high heat, melt butter and olive oil. Add asparagus, red pepper, salt, and pepper and cook, stirring occasionally, for 5 minutes or until vegetables are crisp-tender. Reduce heat. Add flour and cook for another minute, stirring continuously as you add the milk and the peas. Continue to cook, stirring often, until the mixture slightly thickens. Toss the pasta and the green beans together with the sauce and serve with Parmesan cheese and black pepper sprinkled on top.

Tuna Quiche

YOU WILL NEED

1 can of tuna, mashed

½ c. mayonnaise

2 eggs

2 T. flour

½ c. milk

8 oz. grated cheese

1 tsp. garlic powder

Salt and pepper, to taste

1 baked pie crust

START COOKING

In a medium-size mixing bowl, combine tuna, mayonnaise, eggs, flour, milk, grated cheese, and spices. Mix well - the mixture will be lumpy. Pour into baked pie crust and bake uncovered at 350° for 45 minutes.

Mushroom Quiche

YOU WILL NEED

1 (8-oz.) can mushrooms, drained

½ c. mayonnaise

2 eggs

2 T. flour

½ c. milk

1 (8 oz.) bag grated cheese

1 tsp. garlic powder

Salt and pepper, to taste

1 baked pie crust

START COOKING

In a medium-size mixing bowl, combine mushrooms, mayonnaise, eggs, flour, milk, grated cheese, and spices. Mix well and pour into baked pie crust. Bake uncovered at 350° for 45 minutes.

Broccoli Lasagna

SERVES 10–12
(ONE 9x13 PAN)

DAIRY

YOU WILL NEED

2 (8-oz.) bags grated mozzarella cheese (set aside 1 c.)

1 (24-oz.) jar marinara sauce

1 lb. frozen broccoli cuts, defrosted

1 lb. farmer cheese

2 eggs

⅛ tsp. salt

⅛ tsp. pepper

½ tsp. onion powder

½ tsp. garlic powder

1 (9-oz.) box oven-ready lasagna noodles

START COOKING

In a medium-size bowl, combine mozzarella cheese (minus 1 c.) with the marinara sauce and mix well. In another bowl, combine broccoli, farmer cheese, eggs, and spices. In a 9x13-inch pan, begin layering as follows: a thin layer of sauce, four lasagna noodles, broccoli mixture, sauce, and ending with the noodles (repeat as necessary). Sprinkle remaining mozzarella cheese on top. Pour approximately ¼ c. boiling water around the edges of the lasagna, cover well, and bake at 350° for 1 hour.

Baked Cheese and Tomato Pasta Casserole

YOU WILL NEED

4 c. shortcut pasta of your choice,
   cooked until slightly underdone

3 c. grated cheddar cheese

1½ c. grated Parmesan cheese

Salt and pepper, to taste

2 T. butter or margarine

8 T. breadcrumbs

2 T. chopped fresh basil
   (or 3–4 frozen basil cubes)

Sauce:

2 T. olive oil

1 large onion, finely chopped

2 garlic cloves, minced

2 (15-oz.) cans chopped tomatoes

2 T. chopped fresh basil
   (or 3–4 frozen basil cubes)

Salt and pepper, to taste

*Otherwise known as
"Grown-ups' Baked Ziti"!*

START COOKING

In a medium-size pan, heat the oil until hot but not smoking. Add the onion and garlic and sauté for 1–2 minutes. Add the tomatoes, basil, salt, and pepper and cook over medium heat, stirring for approximately 10 minutes. In a small bowl, combine the cheddar cheese with the Parmesan cheese. In a greased 9x13-inch pan, pour a third of the tomato sauce, then a third of the pasta, and then a third of the cheese. Season to taste with salt and pepper. Repeat the layers twice more. Mix the breadcrumbs and basil together and sprinkle over the top. Dot with the butter or margarine and bake uncovered at 350° for 30 minutes or until golden brown and bubbling.

Vegetable Pasta with Basil Cream Sauce

YOU WILL NEED

1 lb. linguine, cooked according to package directions

2 T. oil

1 med. carrot, thinly sliced

1 sm. onion, diced

1 red pepper, sliced into thin strips and cut into 2-inch lengths

1 yellow pepper, sliced into thin strips and cut into 2-inch lengths

1 medium zucchini, thinly sliced

1 c. broccoli florets

1 c. frozen cut asparagus

8 oz. fresh mushrooms, sliced

⅓ c. flour

2 c. cold water

2 tsp. pareve chicken soup mix

½ c. white wine or pareve chicken broth

¼ tsp. salt

¼ c. chopped fresh basil or 4 tsp. dried basil

6 T. grated Parmesan cheese

START COOKING

In a large skillet, heat oil over medium/high heat. Add carrots, onion, peppers, zucchini, and broccoli. Lower heat, cover, and cook for 10–15 minutes. Add asparagus and mushrooms and cook for another 10 minutes. In a pot over medium/high heat, combine flour and water and mix until smooth and no lumps remain. Add chicken soup mix and bring to a boil. Simmer for 2–4 minutes or until slightly thickened. Slowly add wine or broth and salt and continue to stir. Add basil and Parmesan cheese and mix well. Add pasta to vegetable mixture and pour sauce on top. Toss to coat.

Mexican Style Omelet

YOU WILL NEED

3 eggs

2 T. milk

½ tsp. parsley (opt.)

Salt and pepper, to taste

Olive oil or butter, for frying

½ green pepper, diced

½ c. salsa, drained

½ c. shredded cheese

START COOKING

In a small bowl, whisk together eggs, milk, parsley, salt, and pepper, using a metal fork. Heat skillet over medium/high heat until your hand feels warm when held about 2 inches above the surface. Add oil or butter and swirl to evenly coat bottom of skillet. Pour egg mixture into skillet, allowing it to set slightly. Using a spatula, push eggs from edge toward the center. Tilt pan to allow egg to fill spaces. Allow omelet to set approximately 1–2 minutes. In a small bowl, combine green pepper, salsa, and grated cheese. Pour over half of the omelet and gently fold omelet over the filling. Slide filled omelet onto a serving plate.

Cheesy Mushroom Onion Omelet

YOU WILL NEED

3 eggs

⅛ tsp. kosher salt

Olive oil or butter, for frying

1 onion, diced

5 oz. mushrooms, washed and diced

Salt and pepper, to taste

½ c. grated mozzarella cheese

START COOKING

Heat olive oil or butter in a medium-sized skillet over medium/high heat and sauté mushrooms, salt, and pepper for 5 minutes. Add fried onions and continue to sauté for another 5 minutes. Set aside.

In a small bowl, whisk eggs and salt using a metal fork until slightly frothy. Heat a nonstick skillet over medium/high heat until your hand feels warm when held about 2 inches above the surface. Add oil or butter and swirl to evenly coat pot bottom of skillet. Pour into heated skillet and allow to set slightly. Using a spatula, push eggs from edge toward the center, tilting pan to allow egg to fill spaces. Allow to set for 1–2 minutes. Place mushrooms and onion mixture over half the omelet, and sprinkle grated cheese over filling. Gently fold omelet over filling. Slide omelet onto a serving plate.

Greek Omelet

YOU WILL NEED

2 tsp. olive oil or butter, for sautéing and frying

½ c. grape tomatoes, quartered

1 T. scallions, sliced

Pinch of dried oregano

2 T. feta cheese, crumbled

1 T. sliced black olives

2 lg. eggs

⅛ tsp. kosher salt

START COOKING

In a small skillet over medium/high heat, warm 1 tsp. olive oil or butter. Add grape tomatoes, scallions, and oregano and continue to stir until tomatoes have softened, approximately 1 minute. Remove from heat. While still hot, add feta cheese and the black olives and gently mix to combine. In a small bowl, whisk together eggs and salt with a metal fork until small bubbles form. Heat an 8-inch nonstick skillet over medium/high heat until your hand feels warm when held 2 inches above the surface. Add remaining oil or butter and swirl to evenly coat bottom of skillet. Pour eggs into skillet, allowing them to set slightly. Using a spatula, push egg from edge toward the center, tilting pan to allow egg to fill spaces. Allow to set 1–2 minutes. Place tomato and feta cheese mixture over half the omelet and gently fold omelet over the filling. Tilt skillet and slide filled omelet onto a serving plate.

Spinach Lasagna Roll-Ups

A wonderful variation to a regular lasagna recipe — with a far prettier presentation!

YOU WILL NEED

1 (9-oz.) box lasagna noodles, cooked according
    to package directions and cooled
1 lb. frozen chopped spinach, defrosted and drained
2 c. farmer cheese
3 c. shredded mozzarella or cheddar cheese
    (set aside 1 c. for topping)
2 eggs
½ tsp. salt
⅛ tsp. black pepper
2 scallions, finely chopped
1 (24-oz.) jar marinara sauce

START COOKING

In a large bowl, combine spinach, farmer cheese, mozzarella cheese, eggs, salt, pepper, and scallions and mix well until smooth. Place approximately 2 heaping tablespoons of filling into the center of each lasagna noodle and spread to cover entire noodle. Gently roll up and place seam-side down in a greased 9x13-inch pan, packing noodles closely together. Pour marinara sauce over noodles, fully covering their tops. Sprinkle with the reserved grated cheese. Cover pan and bake at 350° for 40 minutes. Serve warm.

Overnight Spinach Manicotti

SERVES 10–12

DAIRY

YOU WILL NEED

1 (8-oz.) pkg. manicotti pasta, uncooked

2 c. farmer cheese

2 eggs

1 (10-oz.) pkg. frozen chopped spinach,
   defrosted and drained

1 c. shredded mozzarella cheese

⅓ c. grated Parmesan cheese

2 T. sugar

¼ tsp. salt

⅛ tsp. black pepper

1 (24-oz.) jar marinara sauce

START COOKING

In a medium-size bowl, mix farmer cheese and eggs until blended. Add spinach, mozzarella cheese, half the Parmesan cheese, sugar, salt, and pepper. Stir the mixture into uncooked pasta shells. Pour half the marinara sauce into a 9x13-inch pan. Arrange stuffed manicotti in a single layer over the sauce. Pour the remainder of the sauce over the shells. Cover tightly and chill in the refrigerator overnight. When ready to cook, bake covered at 350° for 1 hour and 15 minutes. Uncover and sprinkle the remaining Parmesan cheese on top and bake for another 20 minutes. Serve warm.

It's so useful to have impressive recipes you can prepare in advance — and this one is super delicious, too!

Mains
&
Fish

Herbed Baked Fish

SERVES 4

PAREVE

YOU WILL NEED

1½ lb. fish fillet

1 c. leeks, thinly sliced (white part only)

2 garlic cloves, minced

2 tsp. olive oil

8 frozen basil cubes, defrosted

1 tsp. salt

2 plum tomatoes, sliced

1 med. lemon, cut into thin slices

1 lemon (to squeeze over fish)

⅛ tsp. pepper

4 cubes fresh parsley

START COOKING

In a skillet over medium/high heat, sauté leeks and garlic in oil until tender, approx. 5 minutes. Set aside. Mix basil and parsley and place on the bottom of a greased 9x13-inch pan. Carefully place fillets on top. Sprinkle with salt and top with the leek mixture. Arrange tomatoes over the fish and then add the lemon slices. Squeeze juice from the remaining lemon over the whole dish and sprinkle with pepper. Cover tightly and bake at 350° for 30–40 minutes, or until fish flakes easily with a fork.

Pecan Encrusted Salmon

SERVES 4

DAIRY

YOU WILL NEED

4 salmon fillets

2 c. milk

1 c. finely chopped pecans

½ c. flour

¼ c. brown sugar

2 tsp. salt

2 tsp. pepper

3 T. of olive oil

START COOKING

Place salmon fillets and milk into a large Ziploc bag. Seal bag and turn to coat. Set aside for 10 minutes. In a shallow bowl, combine pecans, flour, brown sugar, salt, and pepper. Remove fillets from the bag and shake off any excess liquid. Coat fillets with pecan mixture, gently pressing nuts down onto fish. Heat oil in a large skillet over medium/high heat and fry fillets until browned. Remove from skillet and place fillets on a greased cookie sheet. Bake uncovered at 350° for another 10–15 minutes or until fish flakes easily with a fork.

For those who do not eat fish with dairy, any pareve milk of your choice will work equally well in this recipe!

SERVES 4

DAIRY

Serve with a salad and supper is complete!

Creamy Salmon with Garlic Rice

YOU WILL NEED

1½ lb. salmon fillet

5 T. butter

3 T. flour

1½ c. whole milk

1½ c. shredded cheddar cheese

1 tsp. salt

½ tsp. mustard powder

¼ tsp. dill

Pinch of cayenne pepper (opt.)

3 garlic cloves, minced

1 c. uncooked long grain rice

2 c. chicken broth (or 2 c. boiling
    water combined with 2 tsp.
    chicken soup mix)

START COOKING

In a large pan, melt 3 T. of butter. Stir in flour until smooth. Slowly add milk and bring to a boil. Simmer for 2–3 minutes or until thickened. Add 1 c. cheese, salt, mustard, dill, and cayenne pepper and stir until cheese is melted. Remove from heat. Place salmon in a greased 9x13-inch pan. Pour sauce over fish and top with remaining cheese. Bake uncovered at 350° for 40–50 minutes or until fish flakes easily with a fork. While the fish cooks, sauté garlic and remaining butter in a saucepan until tender, approximately 5 minutes. Add rice and stir for 2–3 minutes. Stir in chicken broth and bring to a boil. Lower heat, cover, and cook for 15–20 minutes or until rice is tender. Serve with the salmon.

Lemon Battered Tilapia with Lemon Butter

YOU WILL NEED

2 lbs. tilapia

1½ c. flour

1 tsp. baking powder

¾ tsp. salt

½ tsp. sugar

1 egg, slightly beaten

⅔ c. water

⅔ c. lemon juice

Oil, for frying

Lemon slices, to garnish

Lemon butter:

3 T. fresh minced parsley (or 6
      frozen parsley cubes, defrosted)

2 garlic cloves, minced

2 T. lemon juice

¼ tsp. salt

⅛ tsp. pepper

1 stick (8 T.) of butter, softened

At the photo shoot for this recipe, food stylist Michael Giletto mentioned a useful tip: To keep batter from "sliding off" fish, dip fish in flour and shake off any excess before coating in batter!

START COOKING

Lemon butter: In a small bowl, combine parsley, garlic, lemon juice, salt, pepper, and butter and mix well. Set aside.

In another bowl, combine 1 c. flour, baking powder, salt and sugar. Set aside. In a large cup, whisk together the egg, water, and ⅓ c. lemon juice. Stir into dry ingredients until smooth. Prepare two plates. Pour remaining lemon juice on one and the remaining flour on the other. Dip fillets in the lemon juice, then dredge in the flour, and then coat with the batter. In a large skillet, heat approximately 1-inch of oil until hot. Lower heat to medium/high and fry fish, a few at a time, for 2–3 minutes on each side or until the fish flakes easily with a fork. Drain on paper towels. Serve fish hot with cold lemon butter.

Teriyaki Salmon

YOU WILL NEED

4 salmon steaks

½ c. teriyaki sauce

⅓ c. honey

2 tsp. oil

2 garlic cloves, minced

START COOKING

Place teriyaki sauce, honey, oil and garlic in a Ziploc bag. Seal the bag and
shake. Add salmon steaks to the marinade and refrigerate for 4–8 hours or
overnight. Pour ¼ c. of the marinade into a 9x13-inch pan and place salmon
steaks on top. (Discard remaining marinade.) Cover tightly and bake at 350°
for 20 minutes. Uncover and bake for another 15–20 minutes or until fish flakes
easily with a fork.

Creamy Dill Baked Fish

YOU WILL NEED

3 lb. fish fillets

1 c. (8 oz.) sour cream

½ c. grated Parmesan cheese

¼ c. butter, softened

¼ tsp. dill

½ tsp. salt

¼ tsp. pepper

¼ tsp. paprika

*Dill and fish pair
wonderfully together!*

START COOKING

Place fish fillets in a greased 9x13-inch pan. In a small bowl, combine sour cream, Parmesan cheese, butter, dill, salt, and pepper. Spoon over fish fillets. Cover tightly and bake at 350° for 30–35 minutes. Uncover and sprinkle with paprika. Bake another 10–15 minutes or until fish flakes easily with a fork.

A tasty, elegant salmon dish fit for any Yom Tov table!

Sesame Salmon

YOU WILL NEED

6 salmon fillets

1½ T. soy sauce

1 T. rice vinegar

1 tsp. garlic powder

1 T. toasted sesame oil

1 T. sugar

½ c. sesame seeds

START COOKING

Place the salmon fillets in a greased 9x13-inch pan. In a medium-size bowl, combine soy sauce, rice vinegar, garlic powder, sesame oil, and sugar and mix well. Pour sauce over the salmon fillets and sprinkle sesame seeds on top. Bake uncovered at 350° for 25–30 minutes or until fish flakes easily with a fork.

APPROX 8 SERVES

DAIRY

Salmon Patties with Dill Sauce

YOU WILL NEED

2 cans of salmon, drained

2 eggs, lightly beaten

1 c. milk

2 T. lemon juice

3 c. crushed saltines (approx. 65 crackers)

2 tsp. finely chopped onion

¼ tsp. salt

¼ tsp. pepper

Dill sauce:

2 T. butter

2 T. flour

1 tsp. fresh dill or ½ tsp. dried dill

¼ tsp. salt

Salt and pepper, to taste

1½ c. milk

START COOKING

In a large bowl, beat the eggs, milk, lemon juice, saltines, onion, salt, and pepper. Add salmon and mix well. Shape into twelve 3-inch patties. Place patties on a greased cookie sheet and bake uncovered at 350° for 30–35 minutes until lightly browned. Meanwhile, melt butter in a saucepan. Stir in flour, dill, salt, and pepper and mix well until smooth. Add milk, a little at a time, and cook stirring continuously for 5–10 minutes or until thickened. Serve with the patties.

Soft and Silky Sweet and Sour Salmon

YOU WILL NEED

6 salmon steaks

1 c. sugar

4 carrots, peeled and cut into chunks

6 fresh lemons, sliced

3 T. salt

1 tsp. black pepper

3 lg. onions, sliced

¼ c. vinegar

4 c. water

START COOKING

In a large pot, combine all ingredients except salmon steaks and bring to a boil over high heat. Place fish into the pot and immediately turn off the flame. (You may have to add hot water to ensure that the fish is fully submerged.) Cover pot tightly and allow to cool. Refrigerate for at least 4 hours before serving.

Freezes excellently! The longer this fish stays in the marinade, the better it tastes!

Moroccan Fish Fillet

YOU WILL NEED

1 lb. frozen fish fillets, defrosted

½ c. oil

2 T. pepper

4 plum tomatoes, diced

½ red pepper, diced

½ green pepper, diced

1 tsp. garlic powder

1 tsp. onion powder

Salt and pepper, to taste

START COOKING

In a large skillet over medium/high heat, combine oil and pepper. Add tomatoes, green pepper, and red pepper and cook for 2–3 minutes. Add garlic powder, onion powder, salt, and pepper and mix well. Place the fish fillets on top and spoon some of the vegetable mixture on top of the fish. Lower flame and cook for another 45 minutes or until fish flakes easily with a fork. Serve fish with the tomato/ pepper mixture spooned on top. Serve warm or at room temperature.

SERVES 8–10

PAREVE

"Tandoori" Gefilte Fish

YOU WILL NEED

1 frozen gefilte fish loaf, cooked
    according to package directions

1 small onion, diced

1 carrot, peeled and diced

2 plum tomatoes, seeded and diced

1 small zucchini, diced

2–4 T. oil

½ tsp. curry powder

1 tsp. garlic powder

Salt and pepper, to taste

START COOKING

In a large skillet over medium/high heat, sauté onions, carrot, tomatoes, and zucchini until soft, approximately 15 minutes. Add the curry powder, garlic powder, salt, and pepper and mix well. Pour over cooked fish loaf. Slice and serve hot or at room temperature.

SERVES 10

PAREVE

Salmon Puffs

YOU WILL NEED

1 (8-oz.) can salmon, diced

2 boxes puff pastry shells

1 (10-oz.) bag frozen spinach,
    defrosted and drained

1 (28-oz.) can French's fried onions

2 eggs

½ c. non-dairy creamer

1 tsp. salt

⅛ tsp. pepper

START COOKING

In a large bowl, combine all ingredients except puff pastry shells and mix well. Put 1–2 T. of mixture into each shell, place on a greased baking sheet, and bake at 350° for 30–40 minutes or until golden brown.

A simple twist to the Salmon Wellington!

A beautifully presented salmon, perfect as a starter or to serve on a large platter as a main dish!

Salmon and Cucumber Lettuce Parcels

YOU WILL NEED

4 smoked salmon portions (sold in vacuum packs; NOT LOX!) or 4 poached or pickled salmon portions

½ English cucumber (or 2 Kirby cucumbers), peeled and sliced

1 T. kosher salt plus ½ tsp. for marinade

6 T. chopped fresh dill

4 T. rice vinegar

2 T. sugar

4 long strips of leek, for tying

4 lg. Romaine lettuce leaves

START COOKING

Place cucumber slices in a strainer and sprinkle with 1 tablespoon kosher salt. Allow to sit for 30 minutes and then rinse well under cold running water. Pat dry with paper towels. Halve each salmon portion horizontally and place the four lower halves in a 9x13-inch pan. Arrange half of the cucumber slices on top of the salmon. In a small bowl, mix together dill, vinegar, sugar, and remaining ½ tsp. kosher salt. Spoon half the dill mixture over the cucumber slices and position the remaining 4 pieces of salmon on top. Layer the remaining cucumber on top of the salmon and top with the rest of the dill mixture. Cover and refrigerate for 24–48 hours. Remove salmon and cucumber from marinade and wrap each portion in a lettuce leaf, securing the bundles with a strip of leek. Spoon the remaining marinade over each bundle just before serving.

Veggie Gefilte Fish

SERVES 8–10

PAREVE

YOU WILL NEED

1 frozen gefilte fish loaf

2 lg. onions, diced

3 carrots, peeled and cut into
   rounds

3 celery stalks, diced

Oil, for sautéing

1 can mushrooms (opt.)

1 (15-oz.) can tomato sauce

4 T. water

½ c. sugar

Salt and pepper, to taste

START COOKING

In a large skillet over medium/high heat, sauté onions, carrots, and celery in oil until soft, approximately 10 minutes. Add mushrooms if using. Add tomato sauce, water, sugar, salt, and pepper. Remove paper from gefilte fish loaf and put into a pot with approximately 1–2 inches of water. Simmer covered for 1¼ hours and then allow to cool. Slice fish and serve warm or at room temperature with a spoonful of sauce on top of each slice.

Fabulous Fresh Tuna Steaks

SERVES 6

PAREVE

YOU WILL NEED

6 tuna steaks (6–8 oz. each)

2 T. olive oil

2 lg. onions, thinly sliced

2 garlic cloves, minced

2 T. red wine vinegar

½ tsp. salt

¼ tsp. pepper

2 tsp. minced fresh parsley, for
   garnish

START COOKING

Heat olive oil over medium/high heat in a medium-size skillet. Add onion and garlic and sauté, stirring occasionally for 10–15 minutes or until onions are translucent. Add vinegar, salt, and pepper and continue to cook, stirring for 2 more minutes. Place tuna steaks in a greased 9x13-inch pan and pour sauce over fish. Cover with aluminum foil and bake at 350° for 15–20 minutes or until fish is opaque throughout but still moist. Sprinkle with parsley before serving.

8-10
SERVES

PAREVE

This is a true winner! It looks so pretty on the plate and offers a change from your regular gefilte fish!

Tri-Colored Gefilte Fish Slices

YOU WILL NEED

1 gefilte fish loaf, fully defrosted

½ salmon gefilte fish loaf, fully defrosted

2 T. vinegar

1 tsp. salt

½ tsp. pepper

½ box frozen dill cubes, defrosted

1 T. olive oil

1 tsp. vinegar

To serve: chrain, mayonnaise

START COOKING

In a small bowl, combine 2 T. vinegar, salt, and pepper. Place regular gefilte fish into a bowl, add half of vinegar mixture and mix well. Divide mixture evenly into 2 bowls. Add dill to 1 of the bowls and mix until thoroughly combined. In a well-greased loaf pan, spread a layer of dill gefilte fish on the bottom and smooth until even. Spread salmon on top and the plain gefilte fish on top of the salmon. Drizzle olive oil and 1 tsp. vinegar over the loaf and bake at 350° for 1 hour and 10 minutes. Serve each slice on a bed of lettuce, drizzled with a mixture of chrain and mayonnaise.

2-4 SERVES

DAIRY

You'll never know the fish is oven-baked — it's as good and satisfying as the deep-fried variety!

Oven Fish and Chips

YOU WILL NEED

Fish:
1 lb. fish fillet
⅓ c. flour
¼ tsp. pepper
1 egg, lightly beaten
2 T. water
⅔ c. cornflake crumbs
1 T. grated Parmesan cheese
⅛ tsp. cayenne pepper (opt.)
To serve: tartar sauce

"Chips":
2 T. olive oil
¼ tsp. pepper
4 lg. potatoes, peeled and cut into ½-inch strips

START COOKING
For "Chips":
In a large bowl, combine oil, pepper, and cut potatoes and toss to coat. Place on a greased baking sheet and bake uncovered at 350° for 1–1½ hours or until golden brown and crisp.

For Fish:
Meanwhile, combine flour and pepper in a shallow dish. On a plate, mix the beaten egg and water. On another plate, combine cornflake crumbs, cheese, and cayenne pepper. Dredge the fish in the flour, dip in egg mixture, and coat with the cornflake crumbs. Place on a greased baking sheet and bake uncovered at 350° for 20 minutes on each side.

Serve with the chips and tartar sauce, if desired.

Crunchy Spicy Tilapia

SERVES 12

PAREVE

A delectable dish that really tastes as good as it sounds!

YOU WILL NEED

6 tilapia fillets, cut in half lengthwise

¾ c. mayonnaise

2 T. lemon juice

4 tsp. garlic powder

1 tsp. paprika

½ tsp. salt

1 tsp. onion powder

1 tsp. red pepper flakes

1 T. water

2½ c. panko crumbs

Cooking spray oil

Garlic Mayonnaise:

2 garlic cloves, minced

1 c. mayonnaise

Sprig of parsley, to garnish

START COOKING

In a small bowl, combine mayonnaise, lemon juice, 3 tsp. garlic powder, paprika, salt, onion powder, red pepper flakes, and water. On a plate, mix crumbs and 1 tsp. garlic powder. Dip each tilapia fillet into mayonnaise mixture and then into crumbs until evenly coated. Place fish on a greased cookie sheet and spray each piece evenly with cooking spray oil. Bake uncovered at 350° for 30 minutes or until fish flakes easily with a fork. In a small bowl, combine garlic and mayonnaise and mix well. Serve fish on individual plates with a little garlic mayonnaise next to each portion, topped with a sprig of parsley.

Desserts

Pecan Pie

8–10
SERVES

PAREVE

Classic and pure bliss!

YOU WILL NEED

1 c. dark corn syrup

3 eggs

1 c. sugar

2 T. margarine, melted

1 tsp. vanilla extract

1½ c. pecans

1 frozen pie crust, unbaked

START COOKING

In a large bowl, mix the first 5 ingredients thoroughly with a spoon. Add pecans and mix again. Pour into pie crust and bake uncovered at 350° for 1 hour.

A chocolate pecan heaven!

Chocolate Pecan Pie

YOU WILL NEED

1 frozen pie crust, unbaked

½ c. flour

1 c. sugar

2 eggs, slightly beaten

¾ stick margarine, melted

¾ c. pecans

¾ c. chocolate chips

1 tsp. vanilla extract

START COOKING

In a large bowl, combine flour and sugar with a fork. Add eggs and margarine and mix well. Add remaining ingredients, except pie crust, until thoroughly combined. Pour into pie crust and bake uncovered at 350° for 40 minutes.

Don't be put off by all the steps — this is truly easy! Try it and see for yourself!

Apple Bomb

YOU WILL NEED

1 c. sugar

1 T. cinnamon

3 Macintosh apples (do not use Red Delicious!), peeled, cored, and quartered

2½ (3.5-oz.) bars pareve Rosemarie chocolate

1 pkg. lg. puff pastry squares, defrosted (10 in a pkg.)

START COOKING

In a small container with lid on, combine sugar and cinnamon by shaking vigorously. Pour mixture onto a shallow plate. Dredge an apple quarter in the mixture and place 2 pieces of chocolate onto the flat part of the apple. Place a puff pastry square on the palm of your hand and gently put the apple on the dough with the chocolate facing up. Drape square over chocolate, ensuring that it is completely encased. Place seam-side down on a greased cookie sheet. Repeat until all dough is used. Bake at 350° for at least 45 minutes or until pastries are puffed and golden. Serve warm with a generous shaking of confectioners' sugar on top of dough.

Chocolate Chip Pie

YOU WILL NEED

6 oz. chocolate chips

½ c. flour

½ c. margarine

½ c. brown sugar

½ c. sugar

2 lg. eggs

1½ sticks margarine, melted

1 baked pie crust

START COOKING

In a large bowl, mix all ingredients except pie crust and chocolate chips until thoroughly combined. Add chocolate chips and mix well. Pour into pie crust and bake at 350° for 1 hour. Serve warm.

An outstanding dessert that will earn you many compliments!

Marbleized Chocolate Oatmeal Squares

YOU WILL NEED

6 T. sugar

6 T. brown sugar

1 stick margarine, softened

¾ c. flour

½ tsp. baking soda

½ tsp. salt

½ tsp. vanilla extract

1 egg

1 c. oatmeal (quick oats or 1-minute oats)

½ c. chopped nuts

1 c. chocolate chips

START COOKING

In a large bowl, cream together sugars and margarine by pressing down with the back of a wooden spoon. Add remaining ingredients except the chocolate chips and mix until thoroughly combined. Press batter into a greased 9x13-inch pan and sprinkle with chocolate chips. Place into the oven for 2 minutes or until the chocolate chips are slightly melted. Remove from oven and marbleize with a metal fork. Bake at 350° for another 25–30 minutes.

These are scrumptious!

Molten Chocolate Chip Ramekins

After searching, trying, and testing for years, the winning recipe is crowned!

YOU WILL NEED

3 c. flour

1 tsp. baking soda

1 tsp. salt

2 sticks margarine, softened

1 c. sugar

1 c. brown sugar

2 eggs

2 tsp. vanilla

½ (10-oz.) bag chocolate chips

Filling:

1 (8-oz.) whipped topping

3 (3.5-oz.) bars pareve
    Rosemarie chocolate

START COOKING

In a medium-size pot over medium heat, mix filling ingredients until smooth. Pour into a container (a Ziploc bag also works!) and place in freezer for ½–1 hour until firm. In a large bowl, combine rest of ingredients, adding chocolate chips last and mix well. Press dough firmly into ramekins until ¾ full. Remove a walnut-size piece of dough, creating a well in each ramekin. Reserve dough. Remove filling from freezer and break off walnut-size pieces; place inside each well. Cover with reserved dough. Bake at 350° for 20–25 minutes or until golden. Serve warm.

Rosemarie Pie

YOU WILL NEED

1 (3.5-oz.) bar pareve Rosemarie chocolate

16 marshmallows

½ c. coffee creamer

1 (8 oz.) whipped topping

1 regular or 8 mini graham cracker crusts

Chopped nuts (opt.)

START COOKING

In a medium-size pot over medium heat, combine chocolate, marshmallows and coffee creamer and mix until smooth. When mixture cools, combine with whipped topping and pour into graham cracker crusts. Sprinkle with chopped nuts, if desired, and freeze. Remove from freezer 30 minutes before serving.

A tantalizing dessert!

Caramel Sauce

YOU WILL NEED

2 T. margarine

1 c. brown sugar

¼ c. coffee (1 tsp. instant coffee dissolved in ¼ c. water)

2 T. corn syrup

START COOKING

In a small pot, melt margarine over medium heat. Add remaining ingredients and mix until thoroughly combined. Simmer for 5–10 minutes and remove from heat. Serve warm over ice cream.

Butterscotch Sauce

YOU WILL NEED

2 T. margarine

1 c. brown sugar

¼ c. coffee creamer

2 T. light corn syrup

START COOKING

In a small pot, melt margarine over medium heat. Add remaining ingredients and mix until thoroughly combined. Serve warm over ice cream.

Chocolate Fudge

YOU WILL NEED

⅓ c. cocoa

⅔ c. sugar

⅓ c. dessert whip

2 T. margarine

1 tsp. vanilla extract

START COOKING

In a small pot, bring the first 4 ingredients to a boil. Add vanilla extract and mix until combined. Serve warm or cold over ice cream.

Hot Chocolate Sauce

8 SERVES

PAREVE

YOU WILL NEED

¾ c. sugar

¾ c. whipped topping

½ c. corn syrup

2 T. margarine

8 oz. chocolate chips

1 tsp. vanilla extract

START COOKING

In a small pot, bring first 4 ingredients to a boil over medium/high heat. Remove from heat. Add chocolate chips and vanilla extract and mix until smooth. Serve hot over ice cream.

6–8 SERVES

PAREVE

Just like the bakery!

Jumbo Chocolate Chip Muffins

YOU WILL NEED

2 eggs

1 c. sugar

1 c. pareve milk

½ c. oil

1 tsp. vanilla extract

3 c. flour

4 tsp. baking powder

1 tsp. salt

1 c. chocolate chips

START COOKING

In a large bowl, whisk eggs and sugar beating vigorously with a metal fork. Add pareve milk, oil, and vanilla and mix until well combined. In a separate bowl, combine flour, baking powder, and salt and mix well. Gently combine wet ingredients with the dry ingredients, being careful not to over mix. Fold in chocolate chips. Grease muffin tin (inside the compartments and all over the top as well) and pour batter into compartments, ensuring that the batter reaches the top of each compartment. Bake uncovered at 350° for 30–40 minutes until golden brown or until a toothpick inserted in the center comes out clean.

2 DOZEN SERVES

PAREVE

Freeze your leftover cake or botched-up batch of cookies as they can always turn into these delicious rum balls!

Rum Balls

YOU WILL NEED

3 egg yolks

2 sticks margarine

3 T. cocoa

3 T. coffee

8 oz. confectioners' sugar

3 capfuls rum extract

3 c. cake crumbs (fresh or from leftover cake or cookies)

Chocolate sprinkles, melted chocolate, chopped nuts, and/or cocoa

START COOKING

In a very large bowl, mix first 7 ingredients together, using your hands. Refrigerate for 2 hours. Form mixture into small balls and dip into your choice of chocolate sprinkles, melted chocolate, chopped nuts and/or cocoa.

Chocolate Chip Ice Cream Cups

YOU WILL NEED

2 sticks margarine, softened

1 c. sugar

1 c. brown sugar

2 eggs

1 tsp. vanilla

1 c. flour

2½ c. oatmeal

¼ tsp. salt

1 tsp. baking powder

1 tsp. baking soda

1 pkg. chocolate chips

START COOKING

In a large bowl, combine all ingredients, adding chocolate chips last. Mix until well blended. Fill well-greased muffin tins ⅔ full and bake at 350° for 15 minutes. Cool completely before removing from tin. *Tip:* The mixture naturally sinks, creating a cavity perfect for a scoop of ice cream! If you wish to serve them warm, remove from muffin tin when cool and reheat on a cookie sheet!

Not Fried Ice Cream (Same Taste!)

YOU WILL NEED

2 c. ice cream, any flavor

1½ c. any crunchy cereal, crushed

2 T. margarine, melted

3 T. honey

⅛ tsp. cinnamon

START COOKING

Place 4 scoops of ice cream in a foil pan. Freeze until very firm, about 2 hours. Combine cereal and margarine in a medium bowl and mix well. Remove ice cream scoops from freezer and roll each scoop in the cereal mixture, coating completely. Return to freezer for at least 1 more hour. Combine honey and cinnamon in a small pan over low heat until hot. Place ice cream on plate and drizzle with honey mixture. Serve immediately.

The key here is to freeze the scoops of ice cream until frozen solid; do not skip this step (as tempting as that may be!) or you will be left with a mess!

10
SERVES

PAREVE

A dessert with style!

Strawberry Crepes and Custard Sauce

YOU WILL NEED

Custard sauce:

1 (8-oz.) whipped topping

1 c. pareve milk

1 instant vanilla pudding

Strawberry Filling:

1 (12-oz.) bag frozen strawberries

3 T. cornstarch

1 c. cold water

1 tsp. lemon juice

1 c. sugar

1 pkg. frozen crepes, warmed or 1 Easy Crepes recipe — see p. 39

START COOKING

Filling: In a medium-size pot, heat ⅔ of strawberries over medium/high heat until it boils. Lower heat and simmer for 5 minutes. In a large pot, combine cornstarch, water, and lemon juice until cornstarch has fully dissolved. Stir in pot until a thick paste is formed. Add sugar and remaining strawberries and mix thoroughly. Cook over low heat for 5–10 minutes or until sugar has dissolved.

Custard sauce: Place all ingredients in a large container with a tight-fitting lid. Shake until thoroughly combined.

Fill crepes with 1–2 T. of strawberry mixture and roll up jelly-roll style. Serve crepes on a plate with a generous amount of custard sauce drizzled on top. Serve warm.

Chocolate Fudge Pie

8-10 SERVES

PAREVE

A slice of decadent chocolate bliss!

YOU WILL NEED

10 T. margarine

1 oz. semi-sweet chocolate chips

6 T. cocoa

2 tsp. instant coffee

3 eggs

1 c. sugar

3 T. corn syrup

1 tsp. vanilla extract

1 frozen pie crust, baked until lightly browned

To serve: chocolate curls, vanilla ice cream

START COOKING

In a small pan over low heat, melt margarine. Remove from heat. Stir in chocolate chips, cocoa, and coffee until chocolate has melted. In a medium-size bowl, beat eggs and sugar with a fork until well blended. Add corn syrup and vanilla extract and mix well. Slowly stir in chocolate mixture until thoroughly combined. Pour into pie crust and bake at 350° for 35–40 minutes or until filling puffs up and forms a crust. When removed from oven, the filling sinks and may crack as it cools; it is supposed to look under-baked. Decorate with chocolate curls and serve with vanilla ice cream.

Elegant but fantastically simple to prepare!

Quick and Easy Apple Tarts

YOU WILL NEED

8 puff pastry squares, thawed
½ c. apricot jelly
4 Macintosh or Granny Smith apples, peeled and thinly sliced

⅓ c. brown sugar
½ tsp. cinnamon
To serve: vanilla ice cream

START COOKING

Place puff pastry squares on a greased cookie sheet. Prick squares with a fork and coat each with a spoonful of apricot jelly. Fan apple slices over the jelly and arrange neatly. In a small bowl, combine brown sugar and cinnamon and mix well. Sprinkle over apples. Bake at 350° for 20–30 minutes or until apples are tender and pastry is golden brown. Serve warm with vanilla ice cream.

This sounds ordinary, but the rainbow of colors creates a seriously magnificent presentation! Bring it to the table and wait for the oohs and ahhhs!

Rainbow Fresh Fruit Trifle

YOU WILL NEED

2 (20-oz.) cans pineapple tidbits, not drained
1 pkg. instant vanilla pudding mix
1 (11-oz.) can mandarin oranges, drained
2 c. strawberries (opt.), sliced
5 kiwis, peeled and sliced
1 bunch purple grapes, cut in half lengthwise
1 bunch green grapes, cut in half lengthwise

START COOKING

In a medium-sized bowl, combine pineapple and vanilla pudding mix and mix until thoroughly combined. Pour into a large trifle bowl and leave to set for 20 minutes. Place mandarin oranges around the perimeter of the bowl and scatter extra ones in the middle. If using strawberries, layer on top of the mandarins. Then layer the kiwi slices, followed by the purple grapes, and finally the green grapes. Refrigerate until ready to serve.

Apple Cherry Strudel

10–12 SERVES

PAREVE

Simply delicious!

YOU WILL NEED

1 flaky pastry dough sheet

1 (21-oz.) can cherry pie filling

3 apples, thinly sliced

½ c. sugar

1 tsp. vanilla extract

Pinch of cinnamon

1 beaten egg, to brush

START COOKING

Unroll dough and pour pie filling evenly over it. In a medium-size bowl, combine apples, sugar, and vanilla extract and layer evenly over pie filling. Roll up jelly-roll style and place on greased cookie sheet, seam-side down. Brush with beaten egg. With a sharp knife, slice diagonal lines halfway down, 2 inches apart. Bake at 350° for 1½ hours or until golden.

Looks stunning on the plate, and is such a refreshing dessert!

Dessert Nachos

YOU WILL NEED

6 flour tortillas

Cooking spray oil

¼ tsp. cinnamon

2 T. sugar

1 c. pareve milk

1 pkg. instant vanilla pudding

1 c. fresh blueberries

1 c. fresh strawberries or frozen in syrup (opt.)

START COOKING

Cut each tortilla into 8 wedges and place on an ungreased cookie sheet. Generously spray tortilla wedges with cooking spray. In a small container with lid on, shake cinnamon and sugar until combined. Sprinkle mixture evenly over tortillas. Bake uncovered at 350° for 10–15 minutes or until lightly browned. Cool. In a small bowl, combine milk and vanilla pudding and whisk vigorously with a fork until thickened. Arrange 6 tortilla wedges, overlapping each other, on each plate. Top with fruit and drizzle pudding mixture on top. Serve immediately.

Out of this world!

Caramel Triangle Heavenlies

YOU WILL NEED

12 graham crackers

3 c. mini marshmallows

1 c. coconut (opt.)

1 c. slivered almonds

¾ c. margarine

¾ c. brown sugar

1 tsp. cinnamon

1 tsp. vanilla extract

START COOKING

Place graham crackers on a greased cookie sheet and top with mini marshmallows. Sprinkle with coconut and slivered almonds. Melt margarine in a pot; add brown sugar, cinnamon, and vanilla extract and mix well. Pour mixture over graham crackers and marshmallows. Bake at 350° for 10–15 minutes until lightly browned and then refrigerate. When cool, cut into 2-inch squares and then cut in half to make triangles.

In Pan Brownies

YOU WILL NEED

2 c. sugar

1 c. oil

6 T. cocoa

1 c. flour

4 eggs

START COOKING

In a greased 9x13-inch pan, combine all ingredients and mix well. Smooth until surface is even. Bake uncovered at 350° for 30–40 minutes.

Have it prepared in the pan, p
it into the oven during the ma
course, and serve a warm squa
along with a scoop of
vanilla ice cream.

Supreme Chocolate Chip Cookies

YOU WILL NEED

1¾ c. oil	2 tsp. baking powder
2 c. brown sugar	4 c. flour
2 c. sugar	2 c. ground oats
4 eggs	2 tsp. baking soda
2 tsp. vanilla extract	24 oz. chocolate chips
1 tsp. salt	

START COOKING

In a large bowl, combine oil and both sugars using a wooden spoon. Add eggs, vanilla extract, salt, baking powder, flour, oats, and baking soda and mix well. Add chocolate chips and mix until well incorporated. Form into walnut-size balls and place on a well-greased cookie sheet. Bake at 350° for 15 minutes or until golden brown.

The ultimate chocolate chip
cookie! They spread out
quite a lot, so make sure you
space them adequately!
This recipe makes a lot of
cookies.

SERVES 1 DOZEN

PAREVE

This is a childhood favorite! You will truly enjoy the crunch and chew!

Chewy Chocolate Crunchies

YOU WILL NEED

4 oz. margarine

4 T. cocoa

4 T. corn syrup

3 oz. sugar

5 c. Rice Krispies or cornflakes

START COOKING

In a large pot, combine all ingredients except cereal. Stir over low heat until smooth. Add cereal and mix until completely coated. Spoon into cupcake holders and cool.

SERVES 10–12

PAREVE

Elegant and a perfect partner to a cup of tea or coffee, or alongside your favorite ice cream.

Chocolate Chip Biscotti

YOU WILL NEED

½ c. sugar

½ c. dark brown sugar

1½ c. flour

½ tsp. baking soda

½ c. oil

1 egg

½ c. chocolate chips

2 tsp. vanilla extract

To serve: ice cream

START COOKING

Combine sugars, flour, and baking soda in a large bowl. Add oil, egg, and vanilla extract and mix well. Add chocolate chips and mix until combined. Form into loaf on a greased cookie sheet. Bake at 350° for 25–30 minutes. When cool, cut into 1½-inch sticks. Serve warm with ice cream.

Lemon Bars

YOU WILL NEED

Crust:

2 sticks margarine, softened

½ c. confectioners' sugar

2 c. flour

Filling:

2 c. sugar

¼ c. flour

4 eggs

6 T. lemon juice

An old-time favorite!

START COOKING

Line a 9x13-inch pan with aluminum foil and grease well. Blend margarine, sugar, and salt. Stir in flour. Spread into pan, pressing evenly to flatten. Bake uncovered at 350° for 20 minutes. In a small bowl, beat all filling ingredients with a metal fork. Pour over crust. Bake uncovered at 350° for 25 more minutes or until no imprint remains when lightly touched in center. Cut into squares and dust with confectioners' sugar.

The Best Soft Chocolate Chip Cookies

2 DOZEN SERVES

PAREVE

These are out of this world!

YOU WILL NEED

4 sticks margarine, softened

1½ c. brown sugar

½ c. sugar

2 pkgs. instant vanilla pudding

4 eggs

2 tsp. vanilla extract

4 c. chocolate chips

4½ c. flour

2 tsp. baking soda

START COOKING

In a large bowl, cream together margarine and both of the sugars with a wooden spoon. Add vanilla pudding and mix until well blended. Add eggs and vanilla extract, mixing until well incorporated. Add flour and baking soda and mix again. Drop cookies by rounded spoonfuls onto a greased cookie sheet. Bake at 350° for 15 minutes or until edges are golden brown (they will look raw in the center). Cool.

10–12 SERVES
(ONE 9x13 PAN)

PAREVE

Another recipe in the pan? Yes, because who likes washing dishes? Enjoy these squares warm or cool; they're delectable any which way!

In Pan Blondies

YOU WILL NEED

2 tsp. vanilla sugar

1 c. oil

2 c. brown sugar

3 eggs

3 c. flour

1½ tsp. baking powder

¾ tsp. baking soda

1 c. chocolate chips

START COOKING

In a greased 9x13-inch pan, combine all ingredients with a fork and mix well. Smooth until surface is even. Bake uncovered at 350° for 40–45 minutes.

Ice Cream Filled Crepes and Chocolate Sauce

SERVES 6

PAREVE

YOU WILL NEED

Chocolate Sauce:

4 oz. whipped topping

½ c. cocoa

½ stick margarine

½ c. sugar

1 pt. pareve vanilla ice cream

1 pkg. frozen crepes, warmed
or 1 Easy Crepes recipe — see p. 39

This is hands down one of the best desserts out there! If you do not have ice cream, just fill with the chocolate sauce or cinnamon and sugar!

START COOKING

In a medium pan over low heat, mix all chocolate sauce ingredients until smooth.

As this is best served warm, keep crepes warm on blech or on top of cholent pot. On individual dessert plates, place crepe and 2 scoops of ice cream. Roll up (no need to tuck ends in) and place seam-side down. Drizzle a generous amount of chocolate sauce across each crepe. Serve immediately.

Jelly Roll

8–10 SLICES SERVES

PAREVE

This is delicious served warm!

YOU WILL NEED

1 c. flour

1 tsp. baking powder

1 T. sugar

Pinch of salt

1 stick margarine, cut into small
   pieces

2 T. soy milk

4 oz. jelly of your choice

Soy milk, for brushing

Sugar, for dredging

START COOKING

In a large bowl, combine flour, sugar, and salt. Rub margarine into flour mixture until it resembles fine breadcrumbs. Add soy milk and mix into a soft dough. Knead dough on a lightly floured surface until smooth and roll into a rectangle approximately 7x9 inches. Spread jelly evenly over the surface, leaving a 1-inch border on one end. Brush the border with soy milk. Roll up starting with the short end. Place carefully, seam-side down, into a well-greased loaf pan. Bake uncovered at 350° for 40–45 minutes. While still warm, brush with soy milk and sprinkle with sugar.

Desserts
&
Dairy

Jumbo Milk Chocolate Chip Cookies

APPROX
20
SERVES

DAIRY

These are truly fantastic cookies!

YOU WILL NEED

2 sticks butter, softened

1 c. sugar

2 eggs, lightly beaten

2 tsp. vanilla extract

3 c. flour

2 tsp. baking powder

2 (3½-oz.) milk chocolate bars, chopped into small chunks (**Tip**: Leave chocolate bars to soften slightly in a warm place before chopping, then chop and chill well before using.)

Sugar, for sprinkling

START COOKING

In a large bowl, cream together butter and sugar using a wooden spoon. Gradually add eggs a little at a time, mixing well after each addition. Add vanilla extract and chocolate chunks and mix. Shape dough into 2 logs. Slice each log into ¾-inch thick rounds and place on a greased cookie sheet. Bake uncovered at 350° for 15–20 minutes or until light golden brown. Remove from oven and immediately sprinkle with sugar.

DAIRY

*Quick, easy,
and impressive-looking!*

In Pan Cinnamon Cake

YOU WILL NEED

2 eggs

½ c. applesauce

1 c. sugar

¼ c. oil

2 c. flour

1 tsp. cinnamon

1 ½ tsp. baking soda

½ tsp. salt

Frosting:

1 (8-oz.) container whipped cream cheese

1 c. confectioners' sugar

1 tsp. vanilla extract

START COOKING

In a greased 9x13-inch pan, mix eggs, applesauce, sugar, and oil until thoroughly combined. Add flour, cinnamon, baking soda, and salt and mix once again. Bake uncovered at 350° for 30 minutes or until a toothpick comes out clean when inserted in the center. Cool.

Frosting: In a medium-size bowl, combine cream cheese, confectioners' sugar and vanilla extract with a metal fork until smooth. Spread frosting over cooled cake.

Butter Pecan Petit Fours

YOU WILL NEED

4 sticks butter, softened

2 c. confectioners' sugar

4 c. flour

2 tsp. vanilla extract

1 c. whole pecans

START COOKING

Using a wooden spoon, cream butter and confectioners' sugar together until smooth. Gradually add flour with a few drops of vanilla extract, mixing well between each flour addition. Pipe or pour mixture into mini cupcake holders. Add a whole pecan into the center of each pastry, place on a cookie sheet, and bake uncovered at 350° for 15 minutes or until lightly golden. Cool.

These cookies are a real treat, rich in taste with a fabulous melt-in-your-mouth texture!

These are seriously one of the most delicious cookies you will ever taste!

Two-Tone Macadamia and Chocolate Chunk Cookies

YOU WILL NEED

1 stick butter, softened

½ c. sugar

½ c. brown sugar

1 egg

1 tsp. vanilla extract

½ tsp. baking soda

1 c. flour

1 c. macadamia nuts, chopped

2 (3.5-oz.) bars of two-tone chocolate, chopped into chunks

(**Tip**: Leave chocolate bars to soften slightly in a warm place before chopping, then chop and chill well before using.)

START COOKING

In a large bowl, cream together butter and sugars using a wooden spoon. Add egg, vanilla extract, baking soda, and flour. In a small bowl, combine nuts and chocolate. Add half of the mixture to the cookie batter, and set the remainder aside. Drop tablespoon-sized balls onto a greased cookie sheet and bake at 350° for 8 minutes. Remove from oven and arrange a few of the nuts and chocolate on top of each cookie. Return to oven and bake for another 8 minutes or until edges are golden brown.

Cannolis with Coffee Liqueur Sauce

YOU WILL NEED

Cannolis:

18 cannoli wafer rolls (e.g., Presidor)

2 (8-oz.) containers cream cheese, not whipped, room temperature

Juice of half a lemon

1 c. sugar

½ c. mini chocolate chips

Sauce:

2 c. vanilla ice cream, defrosted

½ c. coffee or chocolate liqueur

2 tsp. coffee dissolved in ¼ c. hot water

This is a classy dessert that freezes excellently and presents beautifully!

START COOKING

In a medium-size bowl, combine cream cheese, lemon juice, and sugar using a metal fork. Mix well until smooth. Add chocolate chips and pour mixture into a Ziploc bag. Snip off one corner of the bag. Keeping the cannolis in the package, remove the cover and fill them with cheese mixture. Place in refrigerator to set. (Freezes well!)

To prepare sauce: Combine ice cream, liqueur, and coffee in a small bowl and mix well until smooth. Serve 2 cannolis per plate with coffee sauce drizzled on top.

The Ultimate Blueberry Muffin

YOU WILL NEED

Muffin batter:

2 c. flour

1 c. sugar

1 T. baking powder

1 tsp. salt

6 T. margarine, softened

1 egg

⅔ c. milk

1 T. lemon juice

1 tsp. vanilla sugar

1 c. fresh blueberries

Crumb topping:

2 T. flour

2 T. sugar

2 T. margarine, softened

½ tsp. cinnamon

START COOKING

In a large bowl, combine flour, sugar, baking powder, and salt. Add margarine until mixture resembles breadcrumbs. In another bowl, using a metal fork, combine egg, milk, lemon juice, and vanilla sugar and beat slightly. Fold into crumb mixture until smooth (do not over mix!). Fold in blueberries. Spoon batter into a greased muffin tin. In a small bowl, combine all crumb topping ingredients and sprinkle over each muffin. Bake uncovered at 350° for 30–35 minutes or until a toothpick comes out clean when inserted.

12 SERVES

DAIRY

These are truly the only blueberry muffins you will ever make again! The blueberries remain plump after baking and give a fabulous burst of color and flavor!

DAIRY

*Rich and fantastic!
Cheesecake and brownies
are a match made
in heaven!*

Chocolate Cheesecake Brownies

YOU WILL NEED

Cheesecake:

¾ c. sugar

1 (8 oz.) pkg. cream cheese, not
    whipped, softened

1 (8 oz.) sour cream

1 stick (4 oz.) butter, melted

3 eggs, beaten

1 tsp. vanilla extract

3 T. flour

Brownie:

2 (3.5-oz.) bars bittersweet
    chocolate

¾ stick butter (6 oz.)

1 c. flour

2 T. cocoa

½ tsp. salt

1½ c. sugar

3 eggs

START COOKING

Brownie: Melt chocolate and butter in a double boiler until smooth. Remove from heat and add flour, cocoa, salt, sugar, and eggs and mix well. Pour chocolate batter into a greased 9x13-inch pan and set aside.

Cheesecake: In a medium-size bowl, cream sugar and cream cheese until smooth. Using a metal fork to mix, add sour cream, melted butter, eggs, vanilla extract, and flour and whisk until smooth. Pour cheesecake batter evenly on top of the brownie batter. Using the tip of a knife, gently swirl batters together. Bake uncovered at 350° for 40–45 minutes or until a toothpick inserted in the center comes out clean. Allow to cool and then refrigerate for at least 6 hours before serving.

Classic Chocolate Triangle Cheesecake

YOU WILL NEED

Cheesecake:

½ c. sugar

8 T. margarine, melted

1 lb. farmer cheese

Rind from a half a lemon (opt.)

1 egg

1 tsp. vanilla extract

Approx. ½ c. milk, for dipping

2 pkgs. tea biscuits

Topping:

1 c. sugar

6 T. cocoa

4 T. water

2 tsp. coffee

1 stick margarine, cut into small pieces

START COOKING

In a medium-size bowl, combine sugar, margarine, farmer cheese, lemon rind, egg, and vanilla extract and mix well until smooth (it will be a tiny bit lumpy from the farmer cheese). Pour milk into a shallow bowl. Dip biscuits into the milk and immediately place on a large rectangular piece of aluminum foil. Arrange biscuits three across and four down. Spread cheese mixture over biscuits and repeat process twice more, ending with cheese mixture. Place both hands underneath the foil and lift both edges of foil to meet in the top center to form a triangle log. Place in refrigerator.

Topping: In a medium-size pot over medium/high heat, combine sugar, cocoa, water, and coffee and mix well. Bring to a boil, lower heat, and simmer until thickened. Remove from heat and add pieces of margarine. Mix well until fully blended. Cool and pour over cheesecake. Refrigerate for 4 hours or overnight to set.

DAIRY

Double the recipe for a 9x13-inch pan — no matter how much you make of this recipe, you will never have enough!

Crumb Cheesecake

YOU WILL NEED

5 T. of butter, softened

⅓ c. brown sugar, packed

1 c. flour

½ c. sugar

1 (8 oz.) pkg. cream cheese, not whipped, softened

1 egg

2 T. milk

1 T. lemon juice

½ tsp. vanilla

START COOKING

In a medium bowl, blend butter, brown sugar, and flour with a metal fork until mixture resembles coarse crumbs. Set aside 1 c. of the crumb mixture for the topping. Press remaining mixture into an 8x8-inch square baking pan and bake uncovered at 350° for 15 minutes. In a medium-size bowl, combine sugar and cream cheese and mix well until smooth. Beat in eggs, milk, lemon juice, and vanilla using a wooden spoon until well combined. Spread cheese mixture over baked crust and sprinkle with remaining crumb mixture. Bake uncovered at 350° for 25 minutes. Cool and refrigerate for at least 1 hour. Cut into squares.

Mango Pannacotta

6 SERVES

DAIRY

YOU WILL NEED

1½ c. mango nectar

3 T. sugar

1 package of kosher gelatin (11 g)

1½ c. heavy cream

START COOKING

In a medium-size pan over medium heat, bring mango nectar and sugar to a simmer. Remove from heat and stir well to dissolve sugar. Sprinkle gelatin over the liquid, and after a few minutes, stir until it has completely dissolved. Add heavy cream and mix well. Pour mixture through a strainer into 4 glasses or ramekins. Refrigerate 4–6 hours before serving.

A refreshing and elegant dessert!

12 SERVES

DAIRY

Chocolate Cheese Muffins

YOU WILL NEED

Cheese mixture:

8 oz. cream cheese, not whipped, softened

3 T. milk

½ c. sugar

Muffin batter:

2 c. flour

½ c. sugar

3 T. cocoa

4 tsp. baking powder

1 egg, lightly beaten

1 c. milk

¾ stick butter, melted

START COOKING

Cheese mixture: In a medium-size bowl, combine together cream cheese, milk, and sugar (you may have to add more milk) using a wooden spoon until creamy. Set aside.

Muffin: In another bowl, mix flour, sugar, cocoa, and baking powder until thoroughly combined. Add egg, milk, and butter and gently mix until smooth. Do not over mix! Pour muffin batter into a greased muffin tin filling half way. Drop approximately 2 tsp. cheese mixture on top of each muffin and cover with remaining batter. Bake uncovered at 350° for 30 minutes or until a toothpick inserted comes out clean.

Exquisite Out-Of-This-World Cheesecake

10–12 SLICES SERVES

DAIRY

YOU WILL NEED

1 pkg. vanilla cookies, crushed

¼ c. butter, melted

4 c. whipped cream cheese, room temperature

4 eggs

1¼ c. sugar

1 T. vanilla sugar

This is by far the creamiest, most delicious cheesecake you will ever taste! Although it doesn't need it, feel free to decorate it with a topping of your choice!

START COOKING

In a Ziploc bag, combine crushed cookies and butter. Press into a greased 9-inch springform pan. Bake uncovered at 350° for 15–20 minutes. Remove from oven. In a large bowl, beat cream cheese, eggs, sugar, and vanilla sugar using a metal fork until thoroughly combined. Pour over the cookie base and bake uncovered at 350° for 45–50 minutes. (It should look like it is not set in the middle.) Refrigerate overnight before serving.

Cheese Danish Strudel

YOU WILL NEED

2 puff pastry doughs

8 T. apricot jelly

1 white milk chocolate bar

28 oz. whipped cream cheese, softened

½ c. confectioners' sugar

1 egg yolk

1 tsp. vanilla extract

1 egg, lightly beaten, for brushing

1 c. toasted slivered almonds, to garnish (½ c. for each strudel)

START COOKING

Roll out both pieces of dough to approximately 9x12-inch rectangles. Spread jelly evenly over each rectangle. Melt chocolate in double boiler and set aside.

In a medium-size bowl, combine cream cheese, confectioners' sugar, egg yolk, and vanilla extract and mix well. Add melted chocolate and mix again. Spread cheese mixture down the middle of both rectangles, about 3 inches wide. Cut slits 1-inch apart down both sides of the dough until the slit reaches the cheese mixture. Fold top right strip of dough slanting slightly as you bring it over the filling, then fold over the top left strip. Continue folding alternate strips, slanting slightly all the way down and tucking them under at the end. Brush strudels with beaten egg and sprinkle with slivered almonds. Bake uncovered at 350° for 45–50 minutes or until golden brown. Cool and serve at room temperature.

ENJOY YOUR MEALS MADE WITH NO GADGETS!

RIVKY MANIES

JUDAICA
PRESS